THE RIVER WYE

"Welcome home! Above thy head,
Murmuring, sighs the dark yew still.
And upon thy quiet bed,
Softly sleeps the daffodil.

Welcome home! No longer fear —
Evil words nor slanderous tongue;
For the birds but carol here —
Peacefully, their evensong.

CLIENT: ....

JOB: ....

WT No: ....

NAME: ....

DATE: ....

		QTY			QTY
L1P	Min Contact		GTN	GTO Neg Plate	
L2P	9 × 7 Contact		GTP	GTO Pos Plate	
L3P	12 × 10 Contact		KN	Komori Neg Plate	
L4P	18 × 15 Contact		KP	Komori Pos Plate	
L5P	20 × 25 Contact		XPD	Extra Print Down	
L6P	20 × 30 Contact		TINT	use of Master Tint	
AGL1	A3 Agralon		MP1	A4 Matchprint	
AGL2	A2 Agralon		MP2	A3 Matchprint	
AGM1	A3 Agramask		MP3	A2 Matchprint	
AGM2	A2 Agramask		WP	Wet Proof	
STR	Stripping In		OZ	Ozalid	
PLAN	Planning (hrs)				

COMMENTS:

THE RIVER WYE

by

KEITH KISSACK

TERENCE DALTON LIMITED
LAVENHAM . SUFFOLK
1978

Published by
TERENCE DALTON LIMITED
ISBN 0 86138 040 1

First edition 1978
Second edition 1985

Text photoset in 11/12 pt. Baskerville

Printed in Great Britain at
The Lavenham Press Ltd., Lavenham, Suffolk.

Contents

Index of Illustrations

Acknowledgements

ANYONE writing about this river must be indebted to the many specialists who have written in detail about places and matters which he can only touch upon. In this respect I am especially indebted to the researches of Ivor Waters on the lower Wye and W. H. Howse in Radnorshire.

More particularly I must thank the Monmouth and Chepstow Museums, Mr Lynch-Blosse of the Wyedean Tourist Board, The Hereford Herd Book Society and Mr Derek Jones for help with the illustrations; Dr Hunt for information about Bigsweir Bridge; The Kilvert Society for permission to quote from the account of the dawn chorus; Mr M. P. Watkins for lending me Stooke's map; Mr Donald Ward for the canoeing details; Mr K. A. Bradbury for drawing the maps; Mr Otto Maciag for the trouble he has taken over the dust jacket; and my wife and Mr Derek Bayley for reading the manuscript and for their advice and encouragement throughout.

To Audrey

Introduction

GEORGE Borrow, standing on Plynlimon at the source of the Wye, thought it "the most lovely river, probably, which the world can boast of". Bernard Shaw, looking out over its thickly wooden lower reaches towards Chepstow, wrote to Ellen Terry: "If you have never been here it is no use describing this country to you . . . You have not only the ordinary naturalism and freshness of Nature, but a deliberate poetic beauty". And this has almost always been the principal theme of the countless writers who have described a river which meanders for one hundred and fifty-four miles through five of the most beautiful counties in the kingdom.

But, as Borrow realised, "scenery soon palls unless it is associated with remarkable events and men" and, throughout its length, the Wye has been a vital element in the history of the Marches. It rose in Arwystli, flowed along the western border of Gwerthrynion, into Elfael, around the Marcher lordships of Builth, Painscastle and Clifford; into Herefordshire between Grymesworth and Webtree hundreds, along the eastern flank of Archenfield, past Goodrich and Monmouth, between Gwent and the Forest of Dean, and then through the hundred of St Briavels and the lordship of Striguil to the Severn Sea. And not only did it separate Welsh commotes, Saxon hundreds and Norman lordships; it has formed the boundary of parishes, constituencies, dioceses, counties and countries.

In the age of the saints it was the highway for the Celtic missionaries whose names are commemorated in the churches with which they lined its banks. With the coming of the Normans, its castles increased in number and size and the river was integrated into their defences. And, until the turnpikes, the canals and the railways made cross-country travel easier, it was the chief commercial artery between the market towns of the Marches and the sea.

Yet always, the occasional observer, from Drayton to Cobbett, returned to the beauty of the river, so that, in the late eighteenth century, a more detailed study of its course became a deliberate industry. The cult of the Picturesque was based on a set of rules by which the traveller could gain the greatest satisfaction from a vista. It was rather tediously elaborated by its high priest, the Reverend William Gilpin, who decided that the Wye was the most picturesque river for the man of taste to study because of its "mazy course and lofty banks".

The serpentine windings of the river have fascinated writers ever since Drayton, in one of his worst couplets, wrote:

"Meander, who is said so intricate to be,
Hath not so many turns and crankling nooks as she."

But Gilpin found that the constant changes of direction produced a succession of prospects, each in perfect perspective and entirely free from the formality of lines. One effect of his writings was to publicise the Wye Tour as an indispensible requirement for the man of taste. And this, in turn, encouraged the production of a long line of dully repetitive books, occasionally enlivened by aquatints and engravings.

The search for picturesque beauty was obviously open to ridicule. *The Tour of Doctor Syntax* by William Combe, illustrated by Rowlandson, did it boisterously; while Jane Austen, in *Northanger Abbey*, mocked it more delicately when she made Catherine, after listening to a long lecture from Mr Tilney on foregrounds, side-screens and perspective, "reject the whole city of Bath, as unworthy to make part of a landscape".

Although many of the books written on the Wye Tour were illustrated with prints taken from the work of artists of the calibre of Turner, Cotman and Copley Fielding, they were not always topographically accurate. They, even more than the writers, were concerned with the making of a picture and, as Doctor Syntax pointed out,

"Who'er from nature takes a view
Must copy and improve it too."

The Coldwell Rocks. A boat-load of travellers enjoying picturesque scenery.   *Monmouth Museum*

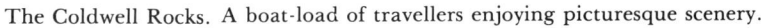

While Jane Austen, thinking more of the enthusiastic amateur, remarked that Fanny's sketches had little bearing on the originals, as she did them while running along the road to keep up with her mother's horse. Even so, the illustrations are often more interesting than the text.

The tour was made in a pleasure boat, rowed by from two to six men. It was equipped with awnings, flags, lockers, vast amounts of food, and a central table at which one wrote, sketched and dined. Those who embarked at Ross spent the first night at Monmouth and reached Chepstow on the second day; for those who started at Hereford the journey took three days, the fare usually being one and a half guineas for each stage. During the Napoleonic wars the tour increased in popularity and, although the decline set in after 1815, there were still people in 1863 doing it the hard way. In that year Prince Arthur, Queen Victoria's third son, aged thirteen, rowed almost all the way from Ross to Chepstow in torrential rain, "doffing his coat and not disdaining to use the oar with his princely hand".

Long before Gilpin introduced the river to the tourist, it had been known to the merchant. Both the Monmouth borough seals, one mediaeval and the other Stuart, show a masted ship to indicate the importance of the Wye in the trade of that town. But the comparatively steep fall of the river, an average of fifteen feet per mile, has always presented difficulties and has meant that a system of locks would have been necessary to make it navigable at all times of the year.

The most comprehensive of many schemes was evolved by Isaac Taylor in 1763. The plan included a series of 22 weirs and locks between Bigsweir and Hereford, each weir throwing the water back to the one above and making it deep enough to take 40-ton barges. It would have cost £20,000 and, needless to say, came to nothing; so navigation has always depended on the amount of water in the river and on the tides below Llandogo. This in turn has led to many quarrels between those who wanted the river kept clear for transport and those who depended on weirs to work mills and forges and, above all, trap fish.

Edward I had tried to keep the river open and, in 1301, a commission had been appointed to inquire into the weirs, dykes and stakes between Hereford and Monmouth "as it appears that boats cannot pass as they were wont". In this case the plaintiff was the city of Hereford, but thirty years later the lord of Monmouth was complaining that the abbot of Tintern had so heightened the weirs on the lower Wye that "ships with wines and victuals and other lading cannot cross to the town of Monmouth and other places adjacent".

The Tintern weirs were important to the monks because, in their early days, the Cistercians would not eat flesh meat and relied largely on fish. It was always the lower Wye that caused the major disputes, since the meanders between Monmouth and Hereford have usually made it quicker to transport small goods overland. The Countess of Pembroke did this in 1296 when a

Bow-hauliers with a barge near Goodrich.   *Monmouth Museum*

barrel of venison was delivered to her at Goodrich by cart, after being brought from Bristol to Monmouth by boat.

Weirs continued to be built (two men were drowned in 1447 trying to repair the one at Monmouth) in spite of protests from upstream. One of the most eloquent advocates of an open river was Rowland Vaughan of Bredwardine. In 1610 he appealed to the Earl of Pembroke to destroy his weirs in the interest of the wine trade: "Good my lord, down with the Weares. Let us have wine with our venison; the carriage of it from London by land makes a cup of claret look like a weake leane wench that hath the greene sickness. And such as we have from Bristowe is fitter to be drunke with a Welche Goate than an English Buck".

Little came of this, although Sir John Scudamore assured Vaughan that "if there were any hope that the overthrow of the Weares would make the river Navigable, Portable or Sammonable, he would pull down his first, to give an instance to others". In 1641 the Herefordshire Grand Jury complained that the weirs were still hindering navigation and at the same time causing "a destruction of the fry of fish".

Once the Civil War was over, schemes to regulate the river by statute began to proliferate, but with little effect on the Wye itself. There were still many private weirs in 1779, and it was not until the nineteenth century that the last of them, the Duke of Kent's at New Weir below Symonds Yat, was demolished.

In spite of the arguments and the difficulties arising from flood and drought, barges full of coal, iron and other goods were dragged upstream, occasionally as far as Hay; while corn, cider and bark in abundance was taken downstream to Bristol and the sea. Most of the goods went in flat-bottomed, keel-less barges, drawing little water and fitted with a mast which could be lowered by winch at the bridges. They had sails but were usually towed upstream by teams of men harnessed by breast-straps to a tow-rope running over a pulley at the mast-head.

H. A. Gilbert, the author of *The Tale of a Wye Fisherman*, was told by one of the last of these bow-hauliers that it was assumed that one man was required for every ton of cargo, and that twenty men were needed to get heavy coal barges upstream. There are several accounts of the hardship the job entailed and, as late as 1847, the *Hereford Journal* described a scene at Brockweir where 32 men were required, harnessed eight at a time in relays, to drag a barge towards Monmouth.

The same paper reported that the difficulties of the bow-hauliers were becoming so great that a steam tug was being considered. A further remedy had been a towpath so that horses could be used; and by 1811 barges, which had previously needed several men, were being towed from Lydbrook to Hereford by two horses. The final solution, a canal from Gloucester to Hereford, had been exercising men's minds for some time.

A Wye barge near Tintern.   *Monmouth Museum*

By 1843 it was within ten miles of Hereford, and when the first coal barges began to use it the local paper announced: "From that day may be dated the desertion of the River Wye as a navigation for the conveyance of foreign produce . . . (They) have given facilities that will probably for ever supersede the Wye . . . for conveyance of Hereford goods". It was unfortunate for the canal promoters that it reached Hereford in 1845, just as the proposal for a railway to Gloucester was being revived.

Although the carriage of coal from Lydbrook was always important to the city of Hereford, it was on the lower Wye that the river traffic was most prolific. The stretch from Monmouth to Chepstow was industrially important from the sixteenth century, when wire works had been established at Tintern and Whitebrook. Small streams, flowing swiftly to the Wye from the heights above, provided cheap power and facilities which were exploited, in the succeeding centuries, in the copper and tinplate works at Redbrook, the paper mills at Whitebrook, and the brass works at Tintern.

Closely linked with Bristol, and getting much of their raw material from the Forest of Dean, the products of these factories were carried downstream in trows and barges which had often been built on the banks at Monmouth, Llandogo, Brockweir and Chepstow. The economic importance of the trade was underlined when the crews, along with those working the Severn barges, were made secure, on paper at any rate, from the press gang.

Although high water was an aid to navigation, flooding brought destruction throughout the river's length. The chief sufferers have been the churches, and the nearness of so many of them to the banks suggests that flooding may have become worse with time, possibly through the felling of the forests and through improved drainage. But whatever the cause there is no lack of evidence for their frequency, or for the damage done by the great floods of 1735, 1795, 1852 and 1947.

Even so, most of the Wye churches have weathered worse perils than water around their sturdy walls. The small, cell-like structures of the Celtic founders were an easy prey for the marauder, Hereford Cathedral itself being burnt and its bishop slain by a mixed force of Danes and Welshmen in 1055. But the sites survived to be rebuilt in stone after the Norman pacification of the border. Finally the Cistercians at Tintern, the Benedictines at Chepstow, Monmouth and Hereford, the Cluniacs at Clifford, and the Augustinians at Flanesford, brought the splendour of Gothic architecture to the banks of the Wye.

Just as the river attracted the conventional merchant, warrior, priest, monk and man of taste, so, at intervals, has it been the haven of the amiable eccentric: Shelley, disastrously married and expelled from Oxford, vegetating above Rhayader; Lady Hester Stanhope mourning for Pitt and Sir John Moore at Builth; the Reverend John Price living in three bathing huts at Painscastle;

The 1929 flood at Dixton.

Monmouth Museum

Kilvert* at Clyro; Traherne at Credenhill; Elgar writing his violin concerto and inventing a new kind of soap at Hereford; John Kyrle at Ross; Charles Rolls ballooning from the Monmouth gasworks; Sidney and Beatrice Webb cycling forty miles from Penallt to attend a trade union meeting at Cardiff; Lord and Lady Amberley preaching birth control and women's suffrage at Cleddon; Antonio Gallenga at Llandogo; the Wordsworths at Tintern; and Doctor Orville Owen dredging the river at Chepstow for the sixty-six boxes of documents which would prove that Bacon wrote Shakespeare's plays.

All of them, whether conventional or eccentric, have felt the enchantment of this river. Even today it remains, over long stretches, unspoilt by unsympathetic development, commercialisation or pollution. It is easily accessible on foot, in a canoe, on a bicycle or by car, but no longer by rail; and it is a sad commentary on our times that one of the most beautiful lines in the country lasted less than a hundred years.

The Great Western Railway had reached Hereford from Ross by 1855 and was continued to Hay in 1864. The Cambrian then opened one of the finest of all lines from Three Cocks to Llanidloes. The Ross to Monmouth section was built in 1874 and continued to Chepstow two years later. Although

*The diarist.

8

these lines eventually killed the river traffic, for a short time the G.W.R. encouraged it by including it in their tickets and time-tables. At the end of the century a third-class return ticket costing 27 shillings covered the rail journey from Paddington to Hereford as well as a boat trip from Hereford down the Wye. The journey could be broken for a holiday anywhere on the river, before taking a boat to Chepstow for the return train to Paddington.

Kilvert, when not walking, used the local trains. In September, 1874, he went on the 10.16 from Hay to Llysdinam and his description of the journey shows well what the motorist, peering anxiously through his windscreen, misses: "I never had a lovelier journey . . . a tender beautiful haze veiled the distant woods and hills with a gauze of blue and silver and pearl . . . I saw all the old familiar sights, the broad river reach at Boughrood flashing round the great curve in the sunlight over its hundred steps and rock ledges, the

Before the coming of the Trunk Road. The old Ross road, the river and the railway at Hadnock. *Monmouth Museum*

luxuriant woods which fringe the gleaming river lit up here and there by the golden flame of a solitary ash, the castled rock-towers and battlements and bastions of the Rocks of Aberedw . . . the house of Pant Shoni gleaming white through the apple-laden orchard trees, the green Castle Mount, Llanvareth Church half-hidden by its great dark yew, the sudden bend of the river below Builth . . . and last but not least the grey-towered house of Llysdinam . . . looking towards the river and the mountains of the South".

With the coming of the railways, travel in its original sense of travail, disappeared. Ruskin considered that going by train was not travel at all and little different from becoming a parcel. But the Wye Valley lines threaded their way through some of the most beautiful country in the kingdom, and anyone who used them for business, for pleasure, or simply to go to school will look back on them with nostalgia. They served a more closely knit community than ours with less sophistication but more friendliness and efficiency than anything that replaced them.

The railways united the valley. One could travel from near Llangurig to Chepstow and remain close to the river. This can still be done, but the car isolates the occupant from the community as the railways never did. The Wye today should be visited on foot, by boat or on a bicycle, preferably in the autumn or spring; and the only excuse for yet another book about it is perhaps best expressed in the words of one who knew it well, Thomas Traherne: "You never enjoyed the world aright till you so love the beauty of enjoying it, that you are covetous and earnest to persuade others to enjoy it".

Wye Valley Railway at Symonds Yat.   *Monmouth Museum*

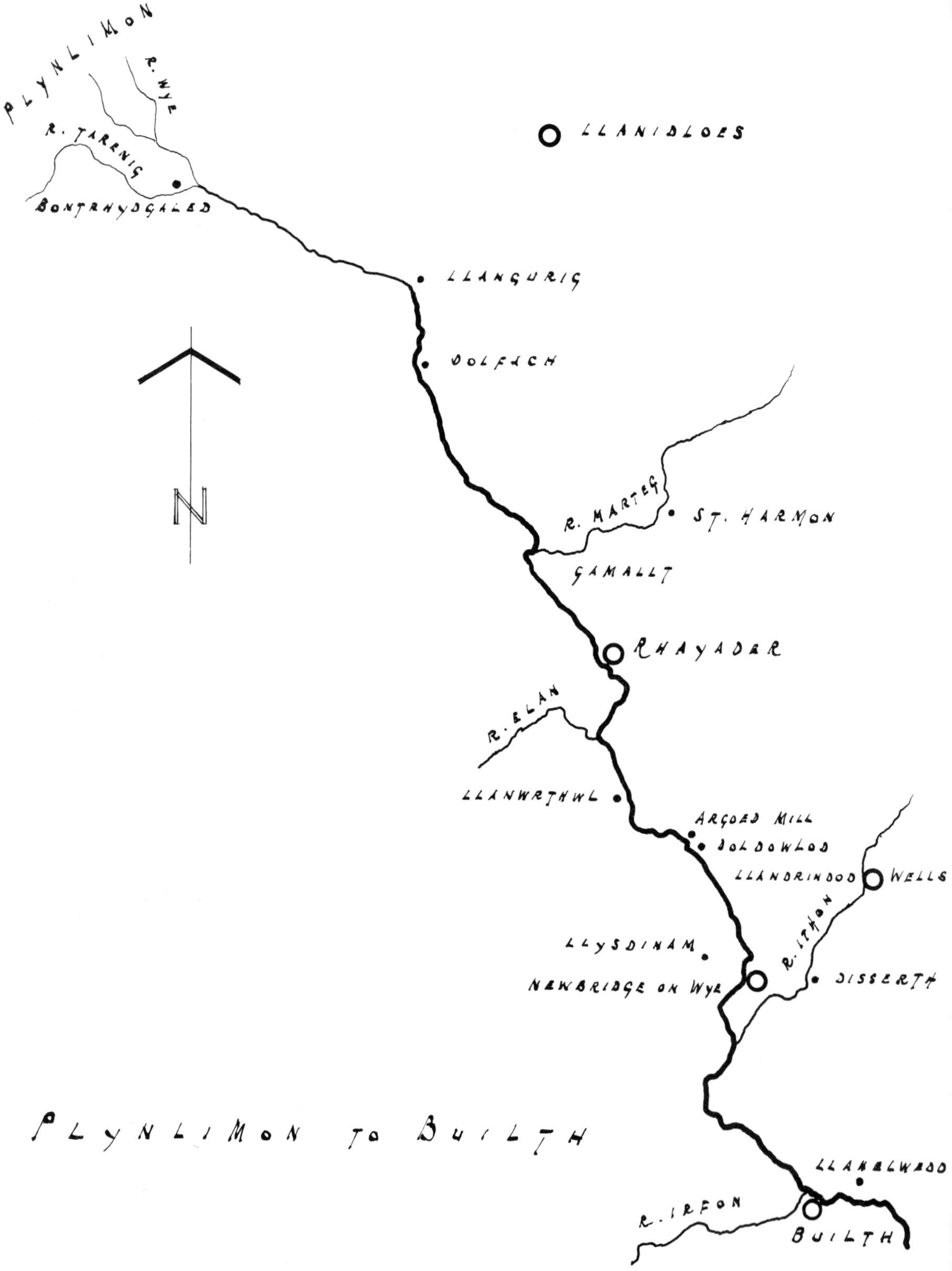

PLYNLIMON

R. WYE

R. TARENIG

BONTRHYDGALED

○ LLANIDLOES

N

● LLANGURIG

● DOLFACH

R. MARTEG ● ST. HARMON

GAMALLT

◎ RHAYADER

R. ELAN

LLANWRTHWL ●

● ARGOED MILL
● DOLDOWLOD
LLANDRINDOD ◎ WELLS

R. ITHON

LLYSDINAM ●

NEWBRIDGE ON WYE ◎ DISSERTH ●

PLYNLIMON TO BUILTH

LLANELWEDD ●

R. IRFON ◎ BUILTH

CHAPTER ONE

Plynlimon to Builth

PLYNLIMON is not a distinctive mountain like Snowdon or Cader Idris. As its name suggests it has five peaks and is the source of the Severn, the Wye, the Rheidol, and many small unnamed rivulets. Walking on it in anything but the driest weather is like treading on a wet sponge; and anyone who has gone there in winter will appreciate the joy with which George Borrow eventually reached the source of the Wye. After drinking copiously, he took off his hat and sang at the top of his voice:

"From high Plynlimon's shaggy side
Three streams in three directions glide,
To thousands at their mouth who tarry
Honey, mead and gold they carry . . ."

When he had finished he explained to his startled guide why Lewis Glyn Cothi equated the Severn, the Wye and the Rheidol with honey, mead and gold.

Borrow thought Plynlimon not much of a hill and his guide agreed that it was not a sociable country, but it has a certain surprising industrial interest in that lead was once mined from its sides. G. H. Malkin, in 1803, was horrified by the unsightly refuse lying about and by "the squalid garb and savage manners of the male and female miners". Indeed, one of the problems of this amazing project was to persuade girls to carry out ore-dressing at 1,600 feet in one of the wettest areas in the country. The Plynlimon lead mines were, in fact, the first serious polluters of the river and, as late as 1872, a writer was complaining about "the lead-poisoned waters of Wye".

Until the reorganisation of local government in 1974 disorganised the maps, the Wye rose in Montgomeryshire, flowed between Radnorshire and Brecon, and its source was on Plynlimon. Now the three counties have been merged into Powys, and it has become fashionable to revert to the accurate but ugly Welsh *Pumlumon*. But as the Wye is an historic river, flows for over half its course through England, and has suffered less change and pollution than almost any other, the old divisions and the English spelling will be retained.

It reaches and passes under the A44, once more nobly known as the Aberystwyth Coach Road, at Bontrhydgaled, and is immediately joined by the Tarenig, a tributary which also rises on Plynlimon, and which, in its early stages, is larger and more impressive than the Wye. It is, perhaps, a feature of this river that many of those who live in the tributary valleys prefer them to the main stream. The Marteg, the Elan, the Yrfon, the Ithon, the Edw, the Lugg and the Monnow all have their devotees, and each has been adjudged more beautiful than the Wye.

From Bontrhydgaled the Tarenig and the Wye, united, flow at the roadside which drops down to **Llangurig** through hills which, on one side, are draped in funereal palls of sitka spruce. With an average rainfall of 61.5 inches and at a height of nearly 1,000 feet, it is not surprising that an early traveller decided that "the voluptuary will find little to detain him in these regions". But Llangurig is a sociable little place, with good pubs, good food and a splendid church.

It was founded in the sixth century by Curig, who came down from Eisteddfa Curig ("the resting place of Curig") on the slopes of Plynlimon, to found a *clas*, or mother church, beside the Wye, which here flows clear and shallow between the stones and coarse grasses of the valley floor. It has a typically solid Radnorshire tower, low and massive, on which Sir Gilbert Scott placed a pleasant but hardly necessary shingle spire in 1877. At this restoration the old screen was reconstructed from drawings, an angel choir was installed, and a series of fine stained glass windows introduced which depict rather unorthodox views on the origins of Celtic Christianity. The chandeliers, like large iron cages, are unusual.

Plynlimon and the Tarenig from Eisteddfa Curig. *The Author*

The Tarenig on Plynlimon.   *The Author*   Near the source of the Wye.   *The Author*

The whole costly scheme was paid for by that eccentric local historian, the *"Chevalier Lloyd"*, from Clochfaen over the bridge. He had been curate of Llandinam, became a convert to Rome, volunteered for service with the Papal Zouaves, (that curious foreign legion formed in 1865 to defend the Papal States), was knighted by the Pope, defected back to the Church of England, and then spent over £10,000 on the restoration of Llangurig.

There is a brass eagle lectern standing on six surprised lions, a fine unexplained panel of embroidery, a font with empty canopies around the bowl (the erasure of the figures, inevitably blamed on Cromwell by the Church guide) and a tablet, with attendant royal crown, attached to the pew on which the future George VI sat when visiting Clochfaen in 1916.

The lych-gate is dated 1740 and the churchyard has a host of fine slate tombstones, one of them, just outside the porch, beginning challengingly:

"Bold infidelity turn pale and die.
Beneath this stone two infants lie.
Say, are they lost or saved?"

It gives the answer at some length.

15

Fuller, in the seventeenth century, called Radnorshire "a chequered county" and, below Llangurig, one sees what he meant. The valley sides are patterned with small fields, rock outcrops, drifts of bracken and isolated farms. Kilvert came to one such farm, Dolfach, high above the river, to see the flowering thorn on Old Christmas Eve in 1875. He found fifteen people clustered round it. Later in the year an old man brought a piece down to Bredwardine and grafted it onto a hawthorn below the terrace. It blossomed in intense frost on Old Christmas Day, nine months before Kilvert died.

The A 470 keeps close to the river and, two miles from Rhayader, the Marteg, one of the Wye's most beautiful tributaries, joins it. This wild valley is worth exploring. It winds up between bare hills to **St Harmon**, a parish of which Kilvert was once briefly vicar. When he first saw the church he thought it simply hideous, and in this he was at one with the churchwardens who, a century earlier, had described it as "a piece of architecture so deformed and so ill contrived yt is very expensive to keep in repair and is chiefly resorted unto by disturbers of divine worship". This was a sad come-down from the twelfth century when, according to Giraldus, it harboured St Curig's gold and silver staff and was a famous place of pilgrimage for those with glandular complaints.

The church was relentlessly restored in 1908 and the bell-turret removed; but there remains a primitive font with four jutting heads, and a nice brass chandelier inscribed "Jas. Haywood Birmingham 1771". The wall monuments at the west end have been cheerfully colourwashed along with the walls and are almost illegible, but on the north wall a 1774 epitaph on a former vicar and his family has the customary ominous invitation to the reader:
"Hark from the Tombs a doleful Sound
My ears attend the Cry
Ye living men come view the Ground
Where you must shortly lie."
Similar sentiments recur in churches throughout the length of the Wye valley.

An attempt was made to establish lead mines at St Harmon in the nineteenth century. One was known locally as "The Old Man's Dream" and the dreamer, Mr Meredith, lies in the churchyard. An earlier threat to the peace of this beautiful valley came from Vortigern whose attempt to find refuge here was foiled through the founder of the church praying for forty days that he would stay away.

Now that even the railway has been closed, it has regained some of the tranquillity which Kilvert enjoyed when, on his first visit, he sat in the churchyard, eating his sandwiches in the May sunshine, alone with the splendid prospect; the stillness of the mountain broken only by the sound of the sheep and the calling of a cuckoo.

CLIENT: .... NAME: ....

JOB: ....

WT No: .... DATE: ....

		QTY			QTY
L1P	Min Contact		GTN	GTO Neg Plate	
L2P	9 × 7 Contact		GTP	GTO Pos Plate	
L3P	12 × 10 Contact		KN	Komori Neg Plate	
L4P	18 × 15 Contact		KP	Komori Pos Plate	
L5P	20 × 25 Contact		XPD	Extra Print Down	
L6P	20 × 30 Contact		TINT	use of Master Tint	
AGL1	A3 Agralon		MP1	A4 Matchprint	
AGL2	A2 Agralon		MP2	A3 Matchprint	
AGM1	A3 Agramask		MP3	A2 Matchprint	
AGM2	A2 Agramask		WP	Wet Proof	
STR	Stripping In		OZ	Ozalid	
PLAN	Planning (hrs)				

COMMENTS:

The Upper Wye.

Wyedean Tourist Board

Llangurig Church.

The Author

The Marteg. *The Author*

The road crosses the Marteg by a bridge (1864) and then turns with the Wye around the hill Gamallt towards **Rhayader**, which *The Thorough Guide* in 1888 described, happily, as "a stand-still little town in a remarkably pretty situation". Earlier in the century Henry Skrine's impression was one of "poverty relieved by unexpected comfort and cleanliness", whereas Thomas Roscoe had found it straggling, ill-lit and dirty. Only George Lipscombe, among the early visitors, commended its food. At the *Red Lion* in 1802 he and his companions enjoyed two roast fowls, a ham, a large dish of veal cutlets, cold roast beef, excellent tarts and a quart of strong beer each. It cost them one shilling a head. Today Rhayader is the nearest thing in Radnorshire to a seaside resort without the sea.

The four main streets are prosaically named from the points of the compass and there is much multi-coloured brick. Neither church has much to offer architecturally, though St Bride's has a good view, through the electricity network, of the famous bridge and falls; while St Clement's has a splendid panorama of the distant hills, but in the foreground, a caravan park, a green footbridge and a bright blue swimming pool.

But the pride of Rhayader has always been its river. It was originally known as Rhaidr Gwy, from the cataract which swept through the town until the channel was widened and the bridge built in 1780. The falls below the bridge are still impressive, and the stretch of water beyond became notorious for the violence of its poaching affrays. Kilvert, in 1878, found the poaching open and peaceful and watched "a large party of Rebeccaites . . . out spearing salmon below Rhayader Bridge . . . a most picturesque sight".

The original Rebeccaites were opponents of the turnpike system, using female disguise and, possibly, taking their name from Genesis where Rebecca's descendants "will possess the gates of them that hate them". Later in the century the same disguise was used by the salmon poachers of the Wye. They eventually became very violent and so successful that in 1907 salmon was being sold in Rhayader for 3d. a pound. The violence coincided with the arrival of the Birmingham Water Works Company to build the reservoirs which were to obliterate so much of two of the Wye's most beautiful tributaries.

The reservoirs were opened by Edward VII in 1904, he and the queen being the first members of the royal family to use the Cambrian line. The waters now cover Nantgwyllt, the house where Shelley once stayed. It had its own chapel and it is alleged that, before it was submerged, the engineers decided to cover the graves with concrete. This led to objections that it was unfair to make it even more difficult for the occupants at the Last Trump.

Rhayader Bridge c. 1820.   *Monmouth Museum*

The Wye above Builth.   *The Author*

Shelley first visited the Elan Valley in 1811 with his friend Hogg. Both had been expelled from Oxford for atheism and both were short of money. A year later Shelley returned with his sixteen year old wife. He tried to buy Nantgwyllt but failed and left with bitter memories of a county in which his grandfather had been High Sheriff and his great-grandfather Lord Lieutenant. He had hoped to make Nantgwyllt "the asylum of distressed virtue, the rendezvous of the friends of liberty and truth". Instead he left complaining that the place was a great bore; "I am now with people who, strange to say, never think . . . I long for a thunderstorm". He found it "quite overstocked with fairies and hobgoblins of every description" but was awed by the scenery. He paid it his tribute in *The Retrospect Cwm Elan:*

"Ye jagged peaks that frown sublime
Mocking the blunted scythe of Time . . ."

Rhayader was the junction of the turnpike roads from Worcester to Aberystwyth and from Builth to Llanidloes and so acquired good coaching inns like the *Cwmdauddwr Arms.* This made it one of the targets of the original Rebeccaites. In 1843 about 150 armed men destroyed four of the six gates and a toll-house. Nowadays Rhayader's invaders come from the Midlands, on their way to what is advertised as The Lake District of Wales, where they can admire the source of the water with which they wash their cars back home.

20

The Elan joins the Wye about two miles south of Rhayader, and for thirteen miles the Builth road accompanies the river through one of its finest stretches. There are few villages, but **Llanwrthwl**, on the right bank, makes a good centre for walking. Kilvert appreciated this, and it was while crossing the Doldowlod suspension bridge, just beyond Argoed Mills, that he was told by Mr George Venables of a conversation with Wordsworth in which the poet had said that he thought the Wye above Hay to be the finest piece of scenery south of the Lakes.

Argoed Mills and the *Vulcan Arms,* just north of it, commemorate a bygone industrialism, and Doldowlod House was, in fact, built by the son of the inventor, James Watt. He bought up several crown manors and tried to eject some of the tenants, action which may have contributed to the ill-feeling which led to the riots of the 1840s.

The road turns away from the river at **Newbridge**, a village with little of architectural interest and too much yellow brick. Kilvert was enthusiastic about "the beautiful little iron church" here, and frequently preached in it. The present building, by S. W. Williams of Rhayader, (he also extended Doldowlod House) is very much a shrine of the Venables family who paid for it. It overlooks the disused railway line, the river and, across the bridge, Llysdinam, the house to which Kilvert's rector at Clyro retired. In 1870 rector

Disserth Church. *The Author*

and curate climbed to the top of Drum-ddu and had marvellous views of the snow-covered slopes of Plynlimon and Cader Idris.

The Ithon, which joins the Wye below Newbridge, has a peculiar beauty which distinguishes it from any other tributary. It also has the disadvantage, when in flood, of bringing down a grey clay, which disrupts the fishing until it subsides. It is a valley worth exploring, if only for **Disserth** church, with its almost unique eighteenth century interior.

The name may have been derived from the Latin *desertum*, but there is nothing Roman about the Celtic dedication to St Cewydd. The large churchyard is circular and, as is usual in Radnorshire, empty of graves on the north side where dances and the parish feast were held. The massive western tower contains the oldest bell in the county and, until the middle of the nineteenth century, also housed the village school.

There is no division between chancel and nave, now that the screen has gone, but the box pews remain, as does the three-decker pulpit, dated 1687. Most of the pews have the initials of the owners or the house to which they belonged, and are dated from 1666 to 1722. The church is white-washed, the floor is flagged, and there are more box pews on either side of the communion table.

The agelessness of Disserth is exemplified by a proclamation giving the times when people suffering from the King's Evil could be presented to Charles II to be touched. It was dated 1683, and was seen, still nailed to the church door, by Jonathan Williams when he was collecting information for the history of Radnorshire in 1815.

The church has the further distinction of having a first-class guide book, written by W. H. Howse in 1952, still on sale.

The railway followed the river between Newbridge and Builth, but the road avoids it. On the left, in the foothills of the Carneddau, is Pencerrig, a house famous for its great oaks which, traditionally, provided the keel of the ill-fated *Royal George,* a ship considered to be the "paragon of beauty and the ultimate of perfection in the science of marine architecture". It sank near Spithead in 1782. Five years later, Thomas Jones that distinctive Welsh painter, a pupil of Richard Wilson, inherited Pencerrig and settled in Radnorshire.

Lechryd church, marked on the map as Cwmbach, stands on the roadside in its immaculate churchyard. It was built in 1877 and is doubly locked by a pleasant grill and a door with exuberant curling strapwork. There was a ford here and the Wye below it becomes turbulent as it meets Builth Rocks.

Kilvert spent a day below the ford in 1875, peacefully reading, "surrounded by the deepening roar of the waters and within a yard of the place where the white plunging foam and the solid mass of deep, clear green water

Builth Parish Church.

The Author

rushed through the narrow rocky channel". He then moved downstream to a quieter stretch where he watched some friends fishing, standing like herons in the river, while a stranger sat watching them from the opposite bank, the four of them linked by silence.

Towards **Builth** the river becomes shallower and broadens as it enters on one of its loveliest lengths. The town grew up around the outer ward of its castle, once one of the most important in Wales, but now no more than a green mound. It was rebuilt in the reign of Edward I by the Master of the King's Works, James of St George, as the strategic centre of a great crown lordship.

It was here that Llywelyn the Last sought refuge in 1282 and was refused admission. Tradition has it that he attended mass in Aberedw church and was then caught near Cilmeri by an English soldier who killed him without knowing his identity. When Llywelyn was recognised, his head was struck off and sent to London. Adam of Usk wrote that the spring where the head was washed "throughout the livelong day did flow in an unmixed stream of blood"; while *Black's Guide*, in 1861, remarked disapprovingly that "the inhabitants have to this day borne the reproachful title 'The Traitors of Builth'".

The town was destroyed by fire in 1691 and appeals were made for help throughout the kingdom but, according to Lewis's *Topographical Dictionary,* enough was received to build only one house. Builth seems to have been similarly unlucky over its parish church which George Cumberland, the friend of William Blake, visited in 1784. He found it "like the rest of the Welsh churches, very little better than a Hogstye". Ten years later an appeal was issued but there was little response and the £800 needed for the rebuilding had to be provided by the parishioners themselves. Although the new church was described as "a neat plain structure", visitors were not impressed by the general appearance of the town and Malkin, in 1803, deplored its "delapidated antiquity" and denounced its main streets for being "as fashionless, as miserable and as dirty" as anything he had ever seen.

The present church was built in 1875. Little was saved from the old building apart from the effigy of Sir John Lloid, "Squire to the body and servant to Our Sovereign Queen Elizabeth", now lying in ignominious discomfort on a stone seat in the porch. Above him is a nice slate tablet (1696) to the mother of five children which is unusual in that, instead of the customary warning to the reader that it is his turn next, it wishes, in simple verses, "long life to them/that do survive".

There is a large churchyard where John Wesley preached, standing on a tomb, with a magistrate protecting him on either side, "and all the people before, catching every word with the most serious and eager attention". This was the first of many such sermons, always preached in the open, presumably due to the opposition of the incumbent. In February, 1784, "notwithstanding

Builth Bridge c. 1820.

Monmouth Museum

the North-East wind . . . more than all the town was gathered in that pleasant vale and made the woods and mountains echo while they sang:

Ye mountains and vales in praises abound,
Ye hills and ye dales, continue the sound;
Break forth into singing ye trees of the wood
For Jesus is bringing lost sinners to God."

The churchyard is now separated from the river by a vast tarmac car park, and the town rises above it to be dominated, not by the massive church tower or the castle ramparts, but by the tall mill-like buildings of the West Breconshire Farmers' Association.

Builth has few outstanding houses. There is a pleasant swan over the entrance to the *Swan Hotel*, but the predominant impression is of the uncompromising brick of Strand Hall and, across the street, its opposite number with an enormous salmon painted on the brickwork and the words "Eadies for felt-bottomed fishing waders". It is a very practical town and the adjective "Fashionless" still applies.

As well as the rather dark brick, there are the slate roofs which so appealed to Kilvert that, looking back ten years, he wrote that "a beautiful enchantment hangs over Builth and the town is magically transfigured still". This is a matter of taste, and others might feel that those roofs, glistening in the rain across the pools of the car park, are short on enchantment. But Builth's importance on a direct line of communication between north and south is marked by its splendid six-arched bridge, built by James Parry in 1779 and widened in 1925.

Lewis Morris, in 1748, said of the Builth wells that, if used externally, they cured cutaneous distempers, and that inwardly they were good for asthma and diseases of the lungs. He complained that the water tasted strongly of sulphur and smelled of gunpowder. There were, in fact, three types, chalybeate, sulphurous and saline, and they became popular again in the 1830s. Two pump rooms were built and, although there was criticism from the infirm that they were too far from the town, sufferers from gout, anaemia, rheumatism, dyspepsia and kidney trouble were assured of their efficacy, if they could travel there.

Lady Hester Stanhope came to Builth to mourn the deaths of Pitt and Sir John Moore, before leaving England for good in 1810. The author of *Tom Shon Catti* lived in the High Street and Hilda Vaughan wrote many of her novels here. But in contrast to these later literary links, Giraldus had trouble over his "treasure store of books" which he was trying to keep out of the hands of the English, by transferring them from Brecon to Strata Florida. His pack-horses were plundered in the mountains of Builth and "in avoiding Scylla, fell into Charybdis". To make matters worse, the books which survived were seized by the monks and he had eventually to abandon them, "feeling as though his very bowels had been drawn from him".

On the Radnorshire side of Builth Bridge, beyond the grounds of the Royal Welsh Show, is the parish of **Llanelwedd**. The church, half a mile from the original site, was restored in 1877. It has a sturdy tower overlooking the river, and some good calligraphy on its tombstones; one, especially graceful, commemorates "a truly honest man", aged eighty-three, and his ninety-three year old wife.

Charles Wesley's wife came from this parish and he wrote "Jesu, lover of my soul" to comfort her old nurse when she was dying. The wedding was performed by John Wesley on a cloudless day, and Charles remembered it as one in which "prayer and thanksgiving was our whole employment. We were cheerful without mirth, serious without sadness. A stranger that intermeddled not with our joy said it looked more like a funeral than a wedding".

Just down the road are the Llanelwedd quarries which supplied much of the masonry for the Elan water works. In so doing they have left a savage wilderness, gouged and blasted from this lovely valley. From Builth to Hay the river is at its most beautiful. The road keeps close beside it for almost all its length, and it was on this road that Wordsworth had his strange encounter with the original of Peter Bell:

"He was a carl as rude and wild
As ever hue and cry pursued,
As ever ran a felon's race . . . "

Not, therefore, a Radnorshire man, if the Reverend Jonathan Williams was correct in his estimation of his countrymen: "They are seldom guilty of those vices with which the inhabitants of many other parts are charged, and possessing health without medicine and happiness without affluence, live contented with the humble station in which Providence has placed them".

Below Llanelwedd. *The Author*

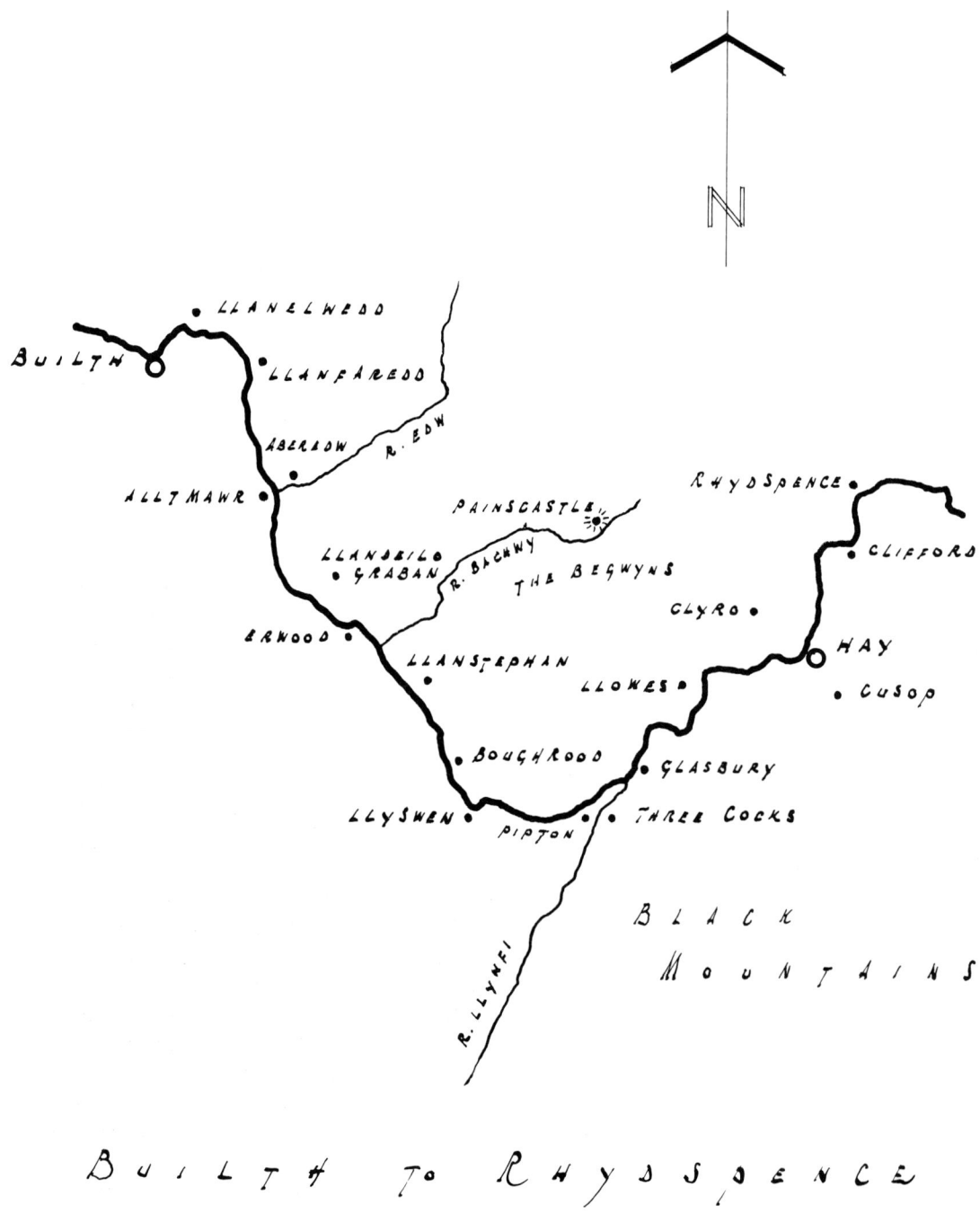

BUILTH TO RHYSSPENCE

CHAPTER TWO

Llanfaredd to Rhydspence

GILPIN considered that the Wye between Builth and Hay was "more beautiful than in any other part of its course", and most people would agree with him. Not least the fishermen, as here are some of the finest of all the great salmon pools: The Hell Hole at Glanwye, The Nith below Aberedw, and Adam's Catch near Three Cocks.

Llanfaredd church, on the left bank, hidden behind the largest yew in the county, which is in turn screened by a farm, is a well-kept little building. It was used as a school in the eighteenth century, and during the 1890 restoration several old exercise books were found under the flooring.

It is white-washed, there are Jacobean communion rails, a large oak chest and the usual pleasant slate tablets by T. Games of Talgarth. The gravestones have been marshalled around the walls of the churchyard, which makes nonsense of a delightful epitaph of 1691: "A Virgin in her blossom nipt Under this stone doth lie". There is another in the porch which states that "In hopes of a joyful resurrection, under the Greene stone there Lyeth the body of Ann ye daughter of Thomas Probert. Aged 12". It is dated 1709. There are other references to "the green stone" in Radnorshire and it is hard to think of an explanation unless it is no more than a poetic reference to the grass in front of the typical upright gravestone.

Llanfaredd was once a chapel-of-ease to Aberedw, and the Reverend Edward Phillips, the man most responsible for bringing Wesley into Breconshire, came from here. There must once have been marvellous views of the river from the churchyard, but now all is hidden by the breeze blocks and corrugated asbestos of an enormous barn.

Five miles below Builth the high hills on the left become castellated with great limestone battlements. The rocks of **Aberedw** produce one of the most impressive of all the scenes on the river. They made Kilvert think of the Gates of Paradise left ajar; "and I may not enter . . . Yet memory enters . . . and again I descend from the high moor's half encircling sweep and listen to the distant murmur of the river . . . Once more I . . . look up at the cliff castle towers and mark the wild roses swinging from the crag, and watch the green woods in the summer afternoon . . . and cross the shining ferry at sunset, when the evening shadows lie long and still across the broad reaches of the river.

Oh Aberedw, Aberedw".

Most of the castle was destroyed when the Cambrian Railway was built and the stones were used in Builth station. But a real village remains with pub, pleasant cottages, and a splendidly intact church. The large churchyard overlooks the Edw, coming steeply down from Llywelyn's Cave. It was a favourite place for parish dances in the eighteenth century, and G. H. Malkin was told by "an intelligent clergyman" that he had seen as many as sixty couples dancing under the great yews on Aberedw Feast (14th June).

The massive timber porch, with its long benches, looks made for sitting-out, while two of the flutes which were used to accompany the choir are still in the church. The chancel is lower than the nave, there is a fine rood screen, slender iron communion rails, flowered commandment boards, and a slate tablet by T. Games, dated 1783, with a timely reminder to the dancers:

"When on this stone you cast your eye
Think of your own mortality.
Remember me you follow must
And lie as I do in the dust."

According to Malkin, the custom of dancing in the churchyard at their feasts and revels was universal in Radnorshire in 1800, as was the playing of fives and tennis against the church walls. But the dancing always took place on the north, the devil's side, where it was considered unlucky to lie, so there was no danger of them dancing on the graves of their forefathers. He considered that the popularity of dancing in this county accounted for the graceful deportment of the women.

This stretch of the Wye is at its most marvellous in the autumn, when the rich red ploughland in the valley and the bracken on the hills blend with the gold of beech, oak and larch along the river. The A 470 accompanies it from Builth to Llyswen, and there are convenient stopping places beneath the trees which overhang the water, running wide and troubled between the rocks.

The inn at **Erwood** has had a mixed press. George Cumberland, who stayed at *The Three Holleys* in 1784, found the accommodation clean, as did Henry Skrine in 1798. He thought it "one of the most delightful spots that can be found by nature . . . Here we found a wonderfully neat house, plenty of rustic fare, and a cheerful old landlady". Roscoe, on the other hand, forty years later, spent one night in it and warned, "Let no other wanderer follow my example". Henry Mayhew, the author of *London Labour and the London Poor,* is said to have taken refuge here from his creditors and to have passed the time laying plans for the founding of *Punch.*

Erwood (*Y rhyd*) means the ford, and it was extensively used by the drovers, bringing their great herds down from the Mynydd Eppynt to drink before crossing and moving on, through Painscastle, to the English border at Rhydspence.

Near Llanfaredd. *The Author*

A mile before reaching Erwood is a bridge leading to Painscastle and **Llandeilo Graban**. There is not much of a village but the fine church of St Teilo stands high above the river, with superb views of the Mynydd Eppynt. Surrounded by great yews and lichen-covered gravestones, it harboured the last Radnorshire dragon, as Mordiford housed the last Herefordshire one. It lived in the church tower, terrorising the neighbourhood, until a ploughboy, attracted by the reward, decided to try his hand at destroying it. He constructed a wooden figure and covered it with knives, hooks and barbs. It was then carefully placed in the tower, near the sleeping dragon. When the beast awoke, it attacked the intruder with such fury that it wounded itself in so many places that it bled to death.

Pinned to the west end is a large tombstone, dated 1772, proclaiming to visitors as they walk up the path, "Diametrically opposite to this stone very much Regretted and Lamented lies Rees Jones . . . A Downright Honest Man". He was eighty-nine, one year older and one degree better than his neighbour at Llanelwedd.

There is a narrow suspension bridge across the river at **Llanstephan**, but the church is isolated high above it. It is worth the climb for the views and the yews. The lych-gate has a room attached, known as The Parson's Chamber, but more probably his horse's stable. There is the usual sturdy tower with a low pyramid roof, a sixteenth century chest, but no sign of "the altar-cloth embroidered by a gentleman" which Ward Lock's *Guide* in 1897 said "will call for attention".

Under the largest yew are the shattered remains of one of the great cast-iron stoves, installed in so many churches to commemorate Victoria's diamond jubilee. It was, presumably, a victim of the rising cost of fuel, although Hereford Cathedral has, and still uses, a regiment of them (Gurney's Patent).

From Aberedw to Rhydspence the river takes a wide sweep to encircle Llanbedr Hill and The Begwns, a remote, mysterious part of Elfael, dominated by the great earthwork of **Painscastle**. Once known as Maud's Castle, after "The Semiramis of Breconshire", as one enthusiast called Maud de Braose, it was rebuilt by Henry III as a base for an attack on Builth. Carpenters were brought from Reading and it acquired a borough, fairs and burgesses. When Kilvert was at Clyro, a mayor of Painscastle was being elected annually. Mr Price, the mayor, assured him sadly that there were "no emoluments, no dignity, no powers".

Only the majestic castle ramparts remain, the last of the stone having been used to build the village school. The church of Llanbedr-Painscastle is about two miles from the village, down the valley of the Bach Howey. It stands in a large, almost circular churchyard, empty of graves on the north side. In the spring it is bright with daffodils. The church was restored in 1879 and is large, plain and light. The original barrel roof of the chancel has been retained and there are pleasant, well-proportioned slate tablets on the walls, one of them coloured.

In 1694 the church was described as being in good repair, with a diligent, resident curate, English and Welsh prayer books, and a suitable churchyard. At the time of the restoration, things were rather different. The vicar, from 1859 to 1895, was the Reverend John Price, a classical scholar of Queen's College, Cambridge and one of the great clerical eccentrics.

Kilvert knew him as a man of about sixty, with luxuriant chestnut hair and moustache and a white beard. He wore a greasy black dress coat, broken shoes, a large cravat and a tall hat. There was no vicarage and he lived first in a small cottage, then in three bathing machines, known as The Huts, and finally, when they were destroyed by fire, in a small grey building which had once been a hen-house. Kilvert went to visit him in this cabin, called Cwm Ceilio, and found inside a wild confusion of litter, books and decaying food; but outside it was "open to the South, and the sun, and the great valley of the Wye, and the distant blue mountains".

He befriended tramps, paid them a small sum to attend services in his church, allowed them to cook their meals there on oil stoves which he provided, and preached to them from notes written in a system of shorthand

Aberedw Church from the castle mound.   *The Author*

Above Erwood. *The Author*

which he perfected and published. For Kilvert's benefit he wrote, in about a dozen strokes, the following verse from a sampler:

"A little health,
A little wealth,
A little house and freedom,
And at the end
A little friend
And little cause to need him."

All who knew him admired his gentle courtesy and kindness. He was known as The Solitary and, as many of those who met him realised, if he had lived a thousand years earlier he would have been revered as a hermit and possibly as a saint. He was eighty-six when he died and the simple cross in Llanbedr churchyard has the words: "For to me to live is Christ and to die is gain".

The Bach Howey flows down the valley from Painscastle to join the Wye just below Erwood. In its lower reaches it plunges down a series of water-falls of which the finest is Craig-Pwll-Du (The rock of the black pool). Kilvert was taken to see it by an old mole-catcher: "Through a narrow rift in the huge black rocks burst a tumultuous mass of snowy foam that plunged forty feet into the black boiling pool below". The mole-catcher told Kilvert that the pool had never been fathomed though attempts had been made. It is still a dangerous place for children.

A branch road comes down from Llanbedr, through the Begwns, to **Boughrood** (the little ford). The church is primly Victorian with its slender spire, red-tiled roof, and black marble gravestones. It is colour-washed inside and abounds in elaborate carving on capitals, string course, pulpit, corbels and brackets. The churchyard, like so many others on the Wye, is thickly planted with wild daffodils, a refreshing contrast to the artifice inside.

It was not always thus. In 1694, except for the royal arms, the church was sadly dilapidated, sermons were rarely preached, there was no vicarage, no school, no surgeon and no midwife. Two centuries later Kilvert was told that it was a miserable place and that the choir sat upon the altar and played a drum.

The Thorough Guide, in 1888, warned that there were no lodgings fit for ladies at either Boughrood or Llyswen, but suggested that the view from the railway bridge was so fine that "a venial trespass should be risked". The bridge carried the Cambrian line from Builth to Three Cocks, a junction which took its name from the inn of that name, "very decent", according to Malkin, "provided the traveller be very modest in his demands". The inn, in turn, seems to have taken its sign from the arms of the Hoskyns family.

The railway has gone, and a road bridge links Boughrood with **Llyswen**, and at the same time, two of the most beautiful counties in Wales. There is a toll-house by the bridge and a compact village with fine trees, white houses and St Gwendoline's church, Victorian inside but with pleasant tombs in the churchyard. One of them commemorates a victim of the river:

"Heedless and harmless as I crossed

The stream that fatal prov'd to me;

In the deep ford this world I lost

And landed in Eternity."

Wordsworth came to Llyswen with his sister Dorothy in 1798. They visited John Thelwall, the radical, who had been tried for sedition in 1794. After his acquittal he had settled for a short time at Llyswen Farm.

At Llyswen the river makes a horse-shoe bend and then turns east again in a wide sweep towards **Glasbury**, which was once partly in Radnorshire and partly in Brecon, but is now wholly in Powys. Between the river and the road is Pipton where, in 1265, Llywelyn the Last signed a treaty with Simon de Montfort who then held the king prisoner. After the signing, Simon, shortly to die at Evesham, returned to Hereford, while Llywelyn and the Welsh lords turned north to lay waste Maud's Castle.

Glasbury is a large village and Lewis's *Topographical Dictionary* talked of its "numerous elegant and genteel houses". There were three hundred of them when Edward Llwyd was collecting his Parochialia, but more than most Wye villages, it has suffered from recurrent flooding. It is also one of the few to have done something about this threat. In 1561 every tenant of the manor living near the river was ordered to plant three rows of osiers, alders or poplars along the bank. Defaulters were to be fined £5 for every rood unplanted.

It was not a success, and in mid-seventeenth century, the church, a Welsh *clas* foundation of St Cynidr, was destroyed, "the churchyard (well nigh) to the very church door, consumed and washed away, the graves opened and the bones carried away". A new site was chosen, high on the Brecon road, and the building was completed in 1664. It was consecrated by the bishop in the following year when the donor of the land symbolised his gift by handing the bishop a freshly dug turf.

The bishop then let the congregation know that it was not enough to attribute the destruction of the old church to the Almighty. Their own behaviour was not blameless and could be improved: "From henceforth there must be none of your parish feasts, nor law courts, nor mustering of soldiers, nor prophane and common uses be exercised. Nay, this place must not be abused . . . ".

Thomas Dineley, visiting Glasbury with the Duke of Beaufort in 1684, called the new church "a plain Country-built fabrick", and so it remained until 1836 when it was taken down and the present one built, with its outsize pinnacles, metal screen and scraped walls. Only the communion rails and a few monuments were transferred from the other church.

There was a great battle here between the Welsh and the Saxons in 1056; later, a Norman castle was held in fee from Clifford by the yearly service of one soar-hawk; and in the nineteenth century Maesllwch Castle, set amongst fine trees and shrubs and with splendid views of the Black Mountains, was built by Robert Lugar, the architect of Cyfarthfa. When Kilvert knew it, the owner kept a baboon which terrorised visitors by jumping from the banisters onto their heads.

As might be expected, there has been a succession of bridges ever since the reign of Elizabeth I. A wooden one was destroyed in 1738. It was followed by another wooden one which was, in turn, replaced by "an elegant stone bridge of seven arches" in 1777. This was washed away in the great flood of 1795, and yet another wooden one was built in 1800. By 1847 it, too, had become unsafe but only after prolonged argument was Breconshire persuaded to repair her half, which she did with stone piers, the Radnor side remaining timber. It has now been replaced by one of the better Wye bridges.

Just beyond Glasbury, on the left bank, a road leads up the hill to Maesyronnen Chapel, the oldest unaltered nonconformist meeting house in Wales. It was built onto an existing farmhouse in 1696. It is a long low building, with pediments over the doors and a sundial. The floor is flagged, there are uncompromisingly upright benches, a coved ceiling and the usual elegant slate tablets, one by William Bowen of Merthyr. It stands high above the Wye, alone with the curlews and lapwings, and is one of the most refreshing survivals on the whole length of the river.

The valley widens as it nears Hay and **Llowes** shelters under the hills on the Radnor side. Giraldus came here in 1196 to visit a hermit and receive his blessing. He called Whethelen "the beloved and elect of God", but others questioned his role in the English attack on the Welsh defenders of Painscastle. His sanctity, however, was sufficient to save him much trouble with his Latin, a language he was unable to master until one day after blessing the bread on the altar, he found he could speak it, although his verbs never got beyond the infinitive.

The present church was completed in 1854 and looks it. There is a large font, bound with iron bands, which was removed from a house in the village; a Georgian royal arms; and one of the few Welsh tombstones in Radnorshire. It commemorates William Bevan who died in 1684 and ends in Latin with "Miserere mei Deus".

Above all, the church contains St Meilig's cross. This is a large stone, carved with a Celtic cross, which, according to tradition, was thrown by Maud Wallbee in a fit of temper when she was building Hay Castle. It landed in Llowes churchyard where it remained until, in 1956, some volunteers and the Llowes Mothers Union moved all three and a half tons of it into the church.

It is not clear what St Meilig, who was a Clydesider, was doing down here, but he chose a marvellous site for his cross. Llowes Common was one of Kilvert's favourite walks, and a year before he died, he came down through the orchards "in greater love than tongue can tell and beauty inexpressible".

Malkin thought that no village on the Wye could be other than pleasing, and in spite of the A 438 which today goes through the middle of it, **Clyro** has much to commend it; a pleasant early nineteenth century pub, a castle moat,

Maesyronnen Chapel. *The Author*

some whitewashed cottages, the memory of a mineral spring which was good for eye diseases, and a church which will always be associated with Kilvert.

He was curate to that even more compulsive diarist, Archdeacon Venables, and they are commemorated in the rather dull church on tablets set side by side, the archdeacon as "Chairman of Quarter Sessions for 25 years" and his curate as "Thou good and faithful servant."

The seven years he spent here inspired Kilvert to some of his happiest memories. From his bedroom at Ty Dulas, now called Ashbrook House, he could look out at Wye Cliff and "the morning spread upon the mountains". It was here that he wrote his poem "Clyro Water", "for seven sweet years my lullaby"; and it was here that he spent his happiest Easter. Walking through the churchyard on Easter Eve, he wrote that the flowered graves looked like people asleep in the moonlight, "ready dressed to rise early on Easter morning". He was up at six, there was a touch of frost, the hedges were yellow with primroses, and he heard the cuckoo for the first time.

The cuckoo usually inspired him; and never more so than when, in 1870, attending a sick mare, he watched over the stable door light growing in the east; "Then I heard a cuckoo near Peter's Pool, then another near Cilblythe . . . It was just cock crowing and the cocks joined in . . . The cuckoos began to call thicker and faster and now and then might be heard from the woods the hooting of the owls. Presently the cocks ceased for a while. Then the owls gradually stopped altogether and the cuckoos had it all their own way. At 3.15 the birds woke and burst into full song, full chorus almost simultaneously . . . No one who has not heard the first marvellous rush of song when the birds awake and begin to sing on a fine warm May morning can have any conception of what it is like . . . " His full description of the dawn chorus on that 7th of May has been published by the Kilvert Society, whose members have placed a sundial to his memory in Clyro churchyard.

John Wesley was once asked to preach in this church but, at the last moment, the vicar changed his mind and he preached instead to a large crowd in the meadow where Kilvert and his friends later held their archery meetings. Howell Harris, however, "an Anglican with a difference", was allowed inside to a service which "fed and strengthened him", in spite of the vicar being "a fighter, swearing drunkard and opposer".

From Clyro, the road leads over the river to **Hay** (it has only recently and pointlessly become Hay-on-Wye), a distance of 1 mile and 75 yards, as a milestone near the bridge proclaims.

Hay has had an unhappy history and, as Ward Lock's *Guide* in 1897 remarked, "Of the tale of its minor catastrophes space will not permit". Giraldus was shocked to find the vicar sharing the offertory with his brother; Glendower laid waste the castle which Maud de St Valerie, traditionally, built single-handed; Leland, who arrived "in crepusculo" and seems to have lost his

Hay Church.   *The Author*

way at the ford, found it "wonderfully decaied"; William Seward, Howell Harris's companion, was murdered outside the *Black Lion*; and Henry Armstrong, the poisoner, once worked in a local solicitor's office.

But the country around, dominated by Hay Bluff, is magnificent, and Henry Skrine, passing through in 1798 on his way back from the north, wrote that "we need not have gone to Scotland in search of the most striking beauties with which Nature has endowed a country".

When Thomas Dineley came here with the Duke of Beaufort in 1684, he described the commodities as "Cotton, corn, cattle, fish and some otter furr". A hundred years later Malkin found that the inhabitants were making flannel and that there was a thread factory. Today it is an unpretentious market town with literary leanings. The rather cramped and aimless streets have some pleasant houses, intermingled with elaborate Victorian shop fronts, one of which, Robert Williams & Sons (1886), has columns of tiles featuring cattle, sheep and pigs, and a row of fearsome plaster faces glaring at the building opposite. Hay is also thick with book shops and advertises itself as having more books for sale per head of the population than any other town. Although most of them have blossomed recently, over a hundred years ago, Kilvert walked from Clyro to attend the annual Book Club sale at the *Rose and Crown*.

The town is dominated by the castle, a considerable mansion, rebuilt in Tudor times, which monopolises the centre. The Lord President of the Marches was handsomely entertained there in 1684; George Psalmanazar, the imposter, is said to have once occupied it; and when Archdeacon Bevan owned it, Kilvert was a frequent visitor, enjoying croquet and archery, and "lawn tea" with the young ladies.

The parish church, which Leland described as "meately fair", well away from the centre of the town and across the ditch of an early motte, has been fiercely restored. It has a pale blue ceiling, highly varnished furniture and prominent electric light fittings. There is a fine tower and porch, and the churchyard overlooks the river.

St John's church, nearer to the centre of the town, has served at various times as guild chapel, school, lock-up, shop, bank and chapel again. It was here that John Wesley preached in 1775 when all the talk was about that curious sect, The Jumpers, who clapped their hands, distorted their features, leaped from the ground and "screamed with all their might to the no small terror of those that were near them".

Like so many Wye towns, Hay has had trouble with its bridges. The first was built in 1763, only to be washed away in the great flood of 1795. Henry Skrine, arriving shortly after this catastrophe, complained of awkward ferries, bad fords and temporary wooden bridges. The temporary bridge survived the 1852 flood which put the gas-works out of action, but was badly damaged by

"The skies in their magnificence, The lively, lovely air" (Thomas Traherne). The Wye between Hay and Bredwardine. *The Author*

ice three years later. It was precariously repaired and, in 1865, was described as a crazy old structure. By then it had been attacked by rioters and the toll gates thrown into the river. A new bridge was designed by Thomas Savin in 1868, and ninety years later the present one, with its curious blue railings, was opened.

The river has been of some commercial importance, being navigable at high water by the flat-bottomed barges which traded with the lower Wye towns. Even the 1740 church bell, aptly inscribed "We move thee to God's Glory", is said to have been brought by barge from Chepstow. Coal, too, came by river until the horse-drawn tramway was opened in 1812. The railway then took its place but, by 1935, a writer was grumbling that coal was coming by motor lorry "and the roads are giving way under the enormous weight put on them, for which they were never intended".

High above Hay, and on the Herefordshire side of the Dulas Brook, is **Cusop** church. It stands in a large open churchyard with fine views. Under one of the yews is the grave of William Seward, the friend of Howell Harris. He had been blinded by a stone thrown in Usk and was killed by one thrown in Hay. The tombstone has the same words as Mr Price at Llanbedr: "To me to live is Christ and to die is gain", and the verse

"If Earth be all
Why o'er and o'er a beaten path
You walk and draw up nothing new
Not so our martyred Seraph did
When from the verge of Wales he fled."

Kilvert has a splendid story about the curate of Cusop arriving late for a confirmation service at Whitney, and being promptly confirmed by the bishop of Hereford who thought he was a candidate. He had the further misfortune to be called Pope.

At Hay the river leaves the dominating Radnorshire hills and the Black Mountains take over. High on the right bank are the remains of the thirteenth century polygonal keep of **Clifford** Castle, the first in a line of fortifications, built shortly after Hastings, for the offensive against Wales. There is not much of it left, but it is remembered as the birthplace of Fair Rosamund, the mistress of Henry II, and the inspiration of much emotional verse:

"Most peerless was her beauty founde,
Her favor and her face;
A sweeter creature in this worlde
Could never prince embrace."

Dryden, alone, brought her down to earth:

"Jane Clifford was her name, as books aver;
Fair Rosamund was but her nom-d-guerre."

There was a Cluniac priory here and the remains are enshrined in Priory Farm, not to be confused with Clifford Priory, a nineteenth century mansion which was destroyed by fire. The church, completely surrounded by trees and well away from the river, has an eighteenth century tower, a dignified oak effigy of a priest, hands folded, in mass-vestments and a sundial on a concrete post advising us to

"Learn from the shadow on the dial
How quick our hours onward move
Be mindful in the state of tryal
Evry moment to Improve."

Torrington, who had complained about reaching Hay "through most horrid roads, but a beautiful country" was delighted with Clifford: "Nothing could equal the beauty of the morning but the pleasantness of the roads". The village has a number of pleasing seventeenth century farms and houses.

Two miles downstream at **Rhydspence** is a sixteenth century inn, once known as *The Cattle Inn*. It was an important collecting centre for the Welsh drovers, whose value to the country was best expressed by Archbishop John Williams when he implored Prince Rupert to allow them safe passage during the Civil War, "for they are the Spanish fleet of Wales which brings us what little gold and silver we have".

Here the oxen were shod for the long journey into England, and here the traveller crosses the border out of Radnorshire, a county not only notable for its beauty, but renowned for the generosity and unaffected politeness of its peasantry. Malkin, in 1804, also noticed that they spoke English "with very few vulgarisms" and remarkably little provincial accent. A. G. Bradley, one hundred years later, confirmed this and agreed that they spoke "the best rustic English in Britain".

The Rhydspence inns were popular with the drovers, and Kilvert, passing through the hamlet at midnight in 1873, found that "the English inn was still ablaze with light and noisy with the songs of revellers, but the Welsh inn was dark and still".

There are fine salmon pools in this length of the river, but the meadows are liable to flooding. There were four inches of mud on the inn floor in 1872, the road was washed bare to the rock, and pigs, sheep, calves, timber and furniture were swept downstream. But the Wye is now in Herefordshire and, flooding or otherwise, assumes a more placid character as it meanders through some of the richest agricultural land in Britain.

The Rhydspence Inn. *The Author*

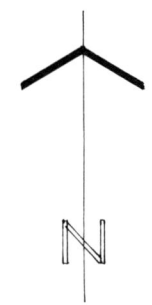

RHYDSPENCE TO HEREFORD

CHAPTER THREE

Whitney to Hereford

THOMAS Fuller, who preferred alphabetical coincidence to accuracy, said of Herefordshire in 1660 that it was noted for Wheat, Wood, Wool and Water. He left out Wine and Women, which Camden included, but acknowledged that, because of its orchards, it would be better named Pomerania.

The river turns east past **Whitney**, a village which has suffered as much from its behaviour as has Glasbury. Glendower is said to have used the ford here before launching his attack on Clifford and the Duke of Beaufort, in 1684, crossed in his chariot. But agitation for a bridge in 1774 led to three being built in quick succession, each in turn being destroyed by flood. A fourth, built early in the nineteenth century, was a toll-bridge. It had a monopoly until the railway arrived, and the toll-owners then managed to persuade the builders of the railway bridge to guarantee the tolls up to £345 a year. The railway bridge has now been demolished and the monopoly has returned to the road bridge which still exacts a toll.

Whitney church and rectory were both swept away in the 1735 flood which altered the course of the Wye and cut a fresh channel. A new church, paid for by the owner of Whitney Court, was built on another site in 1740. Some of the materials were re-used, and the Norman font was salvaged from the old church. The pews and gallery are contemporary and there is a Jacobean reredos dated 1629.

A new rectory was also built, and it was here that the Reverend Henry Dew was incumbent for fifty-eight years. He was an antiquary and collector and is said to have given the reredos to the church. Wordsworth once lunched with him and, on the terrace, which was ever after known as Wordsworth's, remarked (not for the first time) that he had never looked upon a more beautiful scene.

Between Whitney and Letton are several famous salmon pools: Old Court, Locksters, Pikes, The Cowpond and Castleton. It was in The Cowpond, reckoned to be forty feet deep, that in 1923, Miss Doreen Davey caught the record Wye salmon. It weighed 59½ lbs, and measured 52½ inches in length and 29 inches in girth. Clock Mill, on the right bank, was once owned by Raphael Sabatini. There was a ferry here which Kilvert often used on his visits to the Rectory.

It was a great village for celebrating May Day, with a Maypole on the Rectory lawn and the village children's hats garlanded with flowers while they

Kilvert's Vicarage from Bredwardine Bridge.   *The Author*

paid homage to the May Queen. Kilvert noticed that some of the cottages had crossed birch and wittan sprays over the doors "to keep the old witch out".

Between Whitney and Bredwardine the Wye begins its long succession of meanders which prolong its passage through the rich Herefordshire pastures. At **Winforton** there was an island on which St Cynidr, the founder of Glasbury church, had a hermitage and oratory. Winforton church stands in the village, off the main road, with a timber-framed top to the tower. Inside there is a fine eighteenth century organ case, and a large chest, crudely carved in 1722 with the names of the wardens, one of whom is called HIgGINS. An ancestor, Thomas Higgins, gave the pulpit in 1613. One of the panels names him as the donor, while the central one has the roughly carved words "Be not afraide of their faces for I am with thee saith the Lorde". It is not clear to whom the words are addressed — preacher or congregation?

The river then turns north to **Willersley**, one of the most depressing sights on its whole course. The little Norman church lies derelict amongst the rubble of the churchyard, its roofless porch linked by clothesline to a caravan. The south door has a curious Norman lintel, covered with a strange collection of squares, rosettes and zigzags, as if the sculptor had used it to try out his patterns.

One of Wordsworth's friends, John Monkhouse, lived at Stow, and frequently visited him at Brinsop Court. A highly successful farmer, in spite of being almost totally blind for the last thirty-five years of his life, he had read widely and was reputed to know the whole of *Paradise Lost* by heart. He was also one of the first Herefordshire farmers to introduce the threshing machine and as a result was threatened with violence. A letter was found outside the farm promising that "We as you call Rebells . . . will set you and all that you have with fire". It was written in the vein of those sent to the Duke of Beaufort in Monmouth by Captain Swing, but was traced to a local labourer who was transported for fourteen years.

Of **Letton**, Ward Lock's *Guide* remarked, "Nothing is here to attract attention", and today the church is easily missed from the road. It lies amongst farm buildings behind a screen of trees and looks out towards the river. It is well worth visiting for its splendid twelfth century door with huge hinges, its pleasant seventeenth century benches and communion table, and its early eighteenth century pulpit which looks, with its tester, as if it ought to be in a city church. There are several brass tablets to the clergy, one of whom (1697) was married to "a kind wife, a generous housekeeper and a bountiful reliever of the poor". Across the churchyard, the delightful timber-framed cottage was once the rectory.

Letton suffered from the 1795 flood as might be expected. The water was four feet higher in the nave than the oldest inhabitant could remember and sixteen couple of hounds were drowned in the adjoining farm. It is possible that the misfortunes of that year gave rise to the phrase, current in nineteenth century Herefordshire, "Letton-God-help-us".

Bredwardine Church.   *The Author*

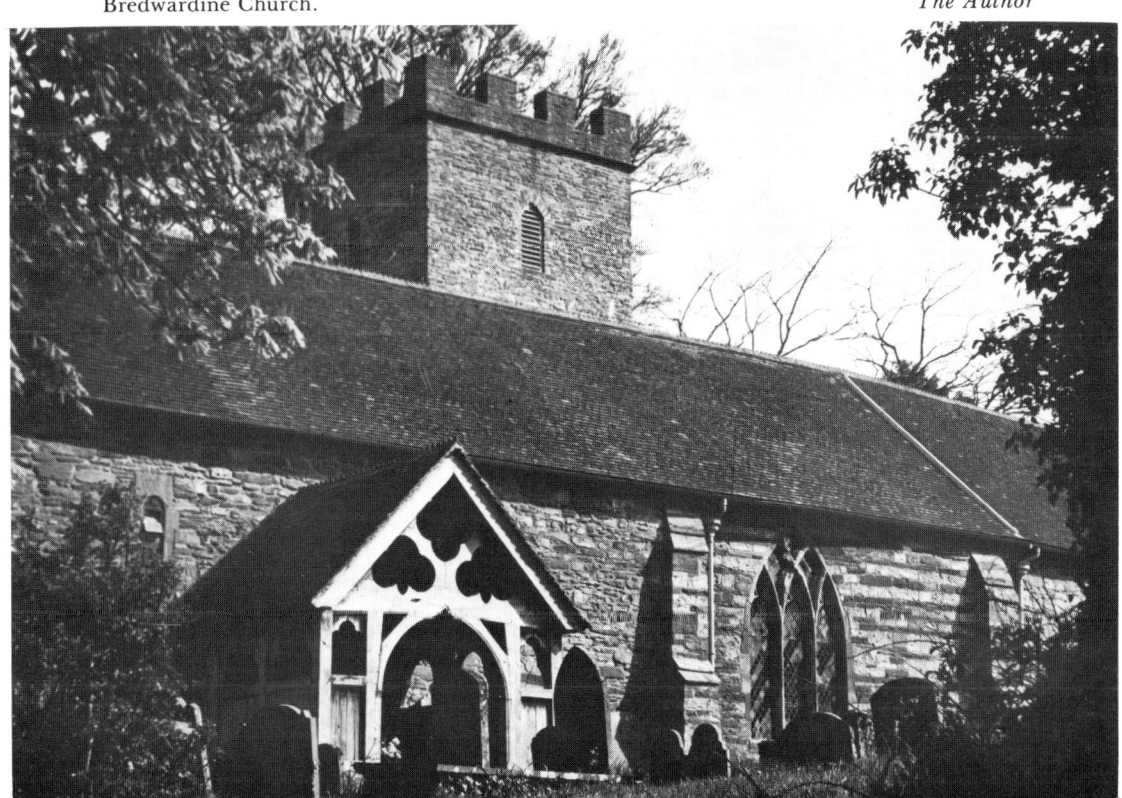

Between Winforton and Willersley the river turns south round Merbach Hill to **Bredwardine** Bridge which, alone on the upper Wye, survived the 1795 flood because the water went over the parapet. Kilvert knew of another flood in which the Hereford coach was wrecked near the bridge because the coachman would not take the bearing reins off the horses and their heads were held under water.

The castle has gone, though the bailey can be traced along the river bank. There are several pleasant houses, including Kilvert's rectory where he lived from 1877 until he died. His kitchen garden was across the river which entailed a half-mile journey to get the vegetables. Nevertheless he entertained generously, a typical tithe dinner given to ten farmers consisting of white soup, roast beef, boiled chickens and ham, curried rabbit, stewed wood-pigeons, beef-steak pie, potatoes and stewed celery, plum pudding, custard, plum tart, mince pies and apricot jam tart.

The church is impressive outside but scraped, varnished and over-restored inside. It has an eighteenth century tower on the north side, possibly replacing an original central one; a fourteenth century chancel, built very askew, as an extension to the original eleventh century building; much early herring-bone masonry; Norman doors (one of which Kilvert knew as the Devil's); an enormous font, and an effigy of a knight in armour of c. 1450, wearing an SS collar and lying with his head on his helm and his feet on an animal.

There is a wall monument in the church to Harriet Thomas who died at the age of sixteen in 1778. It includes the chilling lines:

"God takes the good too good on earth to stay
And leaves the bad too bad to take away."

Kilvert must have known it, and almost exactly one hundred years later, on 13th February 1878, he chose the place for his own grave, "close by the stile leading onto the castle green, beside the path by which the people come to church".

He died of peritonitis soon after getting back from his honeymoon. On the Sunday before he died it was noticed that the bell had a heavy sound, "altogether a different tone from the usual one". The coffin was carried through the arches of flowers which the villagers had put up for the returning honeymoon couple. After the funeral the bells rang "The Welcome Home". He had once written a poem about this chime.

"Welcome home! Above thy head
Murmuring sighs the dark yew still,
And upon thy quiet bed
Softly sleeps the daffodil

48

Welcome home! No longer fear
Evil words nor slanderous tongue;
For the birds but carol here
Peacefully their evensong . . . ''

His grave has the appropriate words, "He being dead, yet speaketh", and there is a seat to his memory under the great yew.

Bredwardine has a pleasant village atmosphere, a real centre, an eighteenth century inn and a delightful setting.

The Wye then passes the site of Trap House ferry and curves round Brobury Scar and its abandoned fourteenth century church to Monnington. Across the orchards, on the left bank, high above the A 438, is the massive tower and pyramid roof of St Mary, **Staunton-on-Wye**. This thirteenth century church has been Victorianised, but there are interesting sixteenth century medallions, and fine views, over the apple trees, to Moccas Deer Park and the hills beyond.

Monnington church and court stand, side by side, across the water meadows from the river which here has shallows through which barges had to be hauled by windlass. Old fishermen maintained that the barge traffic was good for fishing because the keels of the boats scored channels along which the fish could pass. They claimed that these channels silted up when the river traffic ceased and that this affected the fishing upstream.

The church, except for the fifteenth century tower, was built by Uvedall and Mary Tomkins of the Court and their initials and the date, 1680, are on the font. The screen, the communion rails and table, the pulpit, and the

Brobury Scar from Moccas Court. *The Author*

Royal Arms of Charles II, Monnington.
The Author

superb royal arms of Charles II, all have twisted columns, more delicate than those at How Caple, but reminiscent of them. The walls are whitewashed, the benches have open backs, and the plain glass in the windows makes the church wonderfully light.

There is a huge wall monument to Robert Perrott (1667), looking as if he had come straight from the galleys:

"Here Perrott lies whos great capaceous mind
In's Native limits scorn'd to be confin'd.
To th'unknown dangers of enraged seas
And foreigne enemys more feirce than these
His Valor him expos'd. Venice may boast
The aid he lent her to defend her coast
Gainst Unbelieving Turks   thus wisely he
Commits his credit to Posterity."

Kilvert often came to Monnington from Bredwardine, round Brobury Scar, and along Monnington Walk, that splendid avenue of trees which was said to have been planted soon after 1660 to celebrate the Restoration. He referred to it as The Royal Walk in the poem which was found on his desk after he died. He especially enjoyed Sundays at Monnington: "it is so calm and so serene. There is no hurry, no crowd, no confusion, no noise". This must surely still be true.

An iron toll-bridge, with gate designed by John Nash, led over the river from Monnington to **Moccas**. The Court, a fine red-brick house, was built by a local man to the designs of Robert Adam between 1775 and 1781. It has a gracefully curving staircase under an oval dome and a magnificent circular room overlooking the Wye, panelled and beautifully decorated in Etruscan style.

The gardens were laid out by Capability Brown and Humphrey Repton, and beyond, stretching up towards the hills, is the deer park, famous for the great oaks which Kilvert described as "biding God's time with both feet in the grave, yet tiring down and seeing out generation after generation . . . No human hand set these oaks. They are the trees which the Lord hath planted. They look as if they had been at the beginning and making of the world, and they will probably see its end".

Across the park, the small Norman church of St Michael is built largely of tufa, a rock that looks rather like breeze blocks. It is apsidal, with the apse lower than the chancel and the chancel lower than the nave, and beautifully proportioned decreasing arches dividing them. The tympanums over the doors have been eroded, but there is fine fourteenth century glass in the windows which, in the nave, still have the scratchings made by the original masons when setting the jamb-stones. The west end is filled by an enormous organ, installed in 1870, and painted green and gold by Kemp. In such a small church the sound must be impressive to say the least. The chancel is monopolised by a very white effigy of a fourteenth century knight; the Victorian pews are highly varnished; and there is a monument to another victim of the river, Mary Jane Cornewall, "lamentably drowned in the river Wye" in 1839, aged seventeen.

Moccas Deer Park. *The Author*

Moccas Court, 1775-81.   *The Author*

The court, the park, the bridge and the church are all memorials to the Cornewalls, of whom Sir Velters earned the undying gratitude of Herefordshire by opposing in Parliament the taxing of cider and perry. He represented Herefordshire for forty-six years and when he died in 1768 his monument in the cathedral confirmed that "his Unshaken Principles alone directed his conduct in opposing whatever seemed to interfere with the interest of his County".

A relative, Captain James Cornewall, who was born at Moccas in 1698, had both his legs severed by chain-shot when commanding the *Marlborough,* but continued to fight on until he died. In 1756 the first monument to a naval hero in Westminster Abbey was erected in his memory at a cost of £3,000.

After passing under Moccas Bridge, the river flows straight to the Byecross Ferry where it does a double horseshoe turn to **Preston-on-Wye**. When Kilvert visited the church he met the vicar who told him, in the course of casual conversation, that he intended "moving it up to the village green by the old tree where it will be more in the centre of the population". This highly ambitious project evidently proved too much for the vicar, so it was heavily restored instead by Nicholson in 1883. He retained the Norman south door, the Jacobean pulpit, and some pleasant bench-ends attached to Victorian pews.

There is an informative inscription under the tower, carefully carved on a large beam saved from the old church: "THIS CHURCH WAS REEDIFIED THE FIRST YEARE OF THE RAIGNE OF KING CHARLES I ANO DNI 1625". Behind cupboards next to it are some fine slate tablets, one of them (1791) bearing a verse which occurs, with variations, throughout the length of the Wye:

"Sickness sore long time bore
Physicians were in vain
God did adhere my moan to here
And freed me from my pain."

It is a relief to read in the nave a nicely guarded testimonial to Samuel Elliott, yeoman of Preston Court, who died in 1814: "Reader imitate his virtues and draw the mantle of love over his failings, for Perfection is not found in Man".

Ploughfield, about half a mile away, is really more of a village than Preston, but it has come down in status since 1273 when it was classed as a borough, with a bailiff, a market and annual fairs. It lies well away from the river, whereas **Byford**, on the opposite bank, lies close to its ferry. This was an important river crossing and the ferry consisted of two boats with a boathouse, bequeathed by a parishioner during the Civil War. One boat was used for hackneys and cattle and the other "to transfer footmen and such sort".

The church, with its eighteenth century tower and splendid Norman interior, has a fourteenth century painting of St Margaret in one of the transepts, a font dated 1638, a good wall tomb to Uvedale King (1734) by John Jenkins, and some nicely coloured tablets to the Davis family. On the Benefactions board is a grant of money to be distributed amongst "four poor housekeepers on Good Friday". The benefactor (1746) has the splendidly ferocious name of Tamberlane Hords.

The flags of the nave were found, during repairs, to be supported on rows of beautifully constructed short stone piers, similar to those of the Early

Moccas Church.   *The Author*

English arcade. The registers record the planting of the great yew opposite the south porch on February the 2nd in 1744. Its circumference, five feet from the ground, when measured in 1949 was found to be 16' 9". It is now too coated with ivy to make an accurate measurement possible.

The river then turns north to join the A 438 at **Bridge Sollers** where the Norman church has small Romanesque dragons on the imposts of the south door. Two are emerging from a man's mouth to chew his ears, a third is intently watching the worshippers as they enter. The font is dated 1664, there is a pleasing wall monument to William Meats and his wife by Richard Yeoman, and scratch dials on the chancel door. There is some good Victorian glass in the east window and the instruments of the Passion on the reredos.

The hideous bridge is painted a repulsive green.

Not on the Wye, but well worth a diversion to the north of Bridge Sollers, is the small church of **Bishopstone**, isolated next to the moated Court. Much of it is thirteenth century, and it is notable for the delightful woodwork of the chancel roof, the choir stalls, pews and alms boxes (one for the church and one for the poor). There is an imaginatively painted reredos which incorporates features from the seventeenth century onwards, two effigies on a tomb chest of 1614, and a cloying marble monument to Sarah Freer, carved by Peter Hollins in 1842. The gallery at the west end, which formerly held the Father Smith organ from Eton, has been taken down.

A fine Roman mosaic pavement was uncovered when the rectory was being built in 1812. It is illustrated in the Royal Commission volume for Herefordshire, but has since disappeared. Wordsworth was in the neighbourhood when it was found and wrote a sonnet, *Roman Antiquities discovered at Bishopstone*, which begins by putting the archaeologists firmly in their place:

> "While poring Antiquarians search the ground
> Upturned with curious pains, the Bard, a Seer,
> Takes fire . . . "

Just over a mile away, on the old road to Hereford, is the most important Roman town yet found near the Wye, **Kenchester**, or Magna. It enclosed an area of about 22 acres and has been excavated at intervals over the centuries. It intrigued Leland when he visited it, especially the coins found when ploughing, "which the people there calleth Dwarfe's money".

He complained that many houses had been destroyed and used as building material, and he was disappointed in its appearance: "The place where the town was ys al over growen with brambles, hasylles, and like shrubbes. Nevertheless here and there appear ruins of buildings of which the folisch people cawlle one the King of Feyres Chayre . . . To be short, of the decaye of Kenchester Hereford flourished". In another passage he reported that there was "a palays of Offa as sum say". The Roman site seems to have been occupied from the second half of the first century A.D. until the end of the fourth.

The parish church has a delightful Jacobean chancel roof and a curious font which may have been converted from a Roman bowl. There is also Lady Southampton's Chapel, a pleasant red brick building with rounded windows, which was built for the Countess of Huntingdon's Connection in 1830.

Back on the river, at **Canon Bridge**, was a launching pad for logs which were then lashed into rafts to be floated downstream to Chepstow (which had a Raft Street). It was a highly skilled operation, as the rafts were often two "sticks" long and had to be narrow in order to pass through the bridges. The Wye takes another turn to the south at The Weir, Swainshill, a National Trust garden which is at its best in the spring.

Across the A 438 is Credenhill, where Traherne was vicar, and **Stretton Sugwas**, which is not on the Wye at all, but worth visiting for its superb incised slab, commemorating a fashionable couple of c. 1473, the wife wearing a fine butterfly headdress, almost abstract in the geometrical way it has been depicted. Even more worth-while is a magnificent Romanesque tympanum showing Samson astride the lion. His long hair streaming down his back, and a worried look on his face, he is prising the animal's jaws apart like some distracted mediaeval dentist. The lion, its tongue hanging out, has the typical ferocious claws of all the Herefordshire Romanesque lions, but is not using them.

The river, as it approaches Hereford, meanders through rich water meadows, inhabited by Hereford cattle and shaded by fine trees. On the right bank is **Eaton Bishop**, a village with a lot of new housing on the north side and

Stretton Sugwas. Detail from fifteenth century incised slab. *The Author*

an untidy common on the south. The church of St Michael contains the finest fourteenth century glass in the county. Yellow, green and brown, the colours of the Herefordshire countryside predominate, and in summer the cool shade within reflects the trees and the grass of the churchyard outside. The glass was re-set in c. 1850, and again in 1928, and was probably installed by Adam de Murimouth, Canon of Hereford.

Between the village and the river is an Iron Age promontory fort, protected on one side by the Cage Brook, and on the other by the Wye. Across the river, on a similar spur, is another hill fort. Together they guard one of the last fords before Hereford. The Victorian church at **Breinton** has one small Norman window, an unsophisticated monument to Captain Rudhall Booth (1685) and, in the churchyard, a cedar of Lebanon growing over the grave of John Cranston, the founder, in 1764, of the neighbouring King's Acre Nurseries, which here take over from the cattle.

Across the river on the right bank is Belmont Abbey, founded in 1854 and given to the Benedictines, who now run it as a public school. Back on the left bank, at Broomy Hill, is the tall Victorian tower of the Herefordshire Waterworks Museum. This delightful building, which once pumped water from the Wye, contains a fine selection of pumping engines, worked by a hand-fired Lancashire boiler, and is lit by gas at night.

Before reaching the first of the **Hereford** road bridges the river passes some undistinguished urban sprawl and the Hereford Rowing Club's Boathouse. The town regatta is of some antiquity, dating from 1801, twenty-eight years before the first Oxford and Cambridge race. It was an elaborate meeting for four-oared boats, from Wye Bridge to Hunderton and back, and became an annual event under the patronage of the gentry.

The Hereford bridges in downstream order, after the first railway bridge (1853) are: Greyfriars Bridge, pre-stressed concrete in a single span, built in 1965; Wye Bridge, built in 1490; the Victoria Suspension Bridge, built in 1898; and then another nineteenth century railway bridge. But the name Hereford, "the ford of the army", suggests that no bridge was thought necessary until, in the twelfth century at the earliest, a wooden one was built.

That bridge must have been one of the first to be wrecked by the river. Richard II gave thirty oaks and the necessary stone for its repair after it had been "broken and destroyed by the force of the water". He also granted the city the right to levy tolls on all goods crossing the bridge for a period of ten years.

The river affords the best view of the cathedral which, in 1976, celebrated the 1300th anniversary of the arrival of Bishop Putta from Rochester. For most of that time it has dominated the town, but in 1786 the west tower fell into the nave, destroying half of it. The disaster occurred on Easter Monday and the *Hereford Journal* commented that "the ruins though awful, afford a pleasing

Hereford Cathedral.   *Wyedean Tourist Board*

view, especially to behold the statues of kings and bishops resting one upon another".

This rather light-hearted attitude, a multiplicity of architects, and a general lack of urgency over repairs, led to criticism. Fifty years after the disaster Thomas Roscoe found great neglect everywhere, "and where repairs or restorations *are* attempted the very spirit of discord seems to prevail with the directors . . . (they) hide the grandest architectural beauty and the most curious work of ancient art by bran-new painted pews and pert-looking epitaph slabs, destroy whole chapels to save the cost of repairing them . . . and bestow their atrocious malediction of whitewash on all things it can spoil". Memorial brasses seem to have been taken up wholesale and two tons of them were sold to a brazier. The spire was removed from the central tower for safety.

But, in spite of the criticism, much of the original building was retained: the beautiful Lady Chapel and the north transept; the fourteenth century Swinefield monument in the vestibule; the misericords in the choir: the Aquablanca and Cantilupe tombs; the huge Norman font; and the thirteenth century reliquary of St Thomas the Martyr.

There is also the Mappa Mundi, made on vellum by Richard de Bello, treasurer of Lincoln Cathedral, some time after 1280. In a fine mixture of fact

57

and legend it locates The Garden of Eden, The Pillars of Hercules, The Labyrinth, The Colossus of Rhodes, Lot's Wife, The Sphinx, The Phoenix, Olympus, Noah's Ark, camels, crocodiles and elephants, and the Sciapod, lying on his back and shading himself with his one umbrella-like foot from the Asian sun.

The High-Victorian metal screen, made by Skidmore of Coventry, has been returned to that town, after some controversy. But the chained library, containing some 1,444 books and manuscripts going back to the seventh century, has been saved. That this has happened is something of a miracle because, although a muniment room was built back in the thirteenth century, attempts to care for the books have been spasmodic.

Doctor Dee was one of the first recorded visitors, and soon after his visit Queen Elizabeth's commissioners reported that it was in a deplorably dirty state. Thomas Thornton, the precentor, became librarian in 1595, drew up rules, and began to increase the collection. Amongst his acquisitions were twenty-three books which the Dean, who had been chaplain to Essex's expedition against Cadiz, had managed to loot from the Jesuit College there, "jure belli" so he claimed.

In 1842 the books were all in a lumber room of the Vicars' College, but were taken back to the muniment room because the dean warned that unless "the rubbish" was removed it would be burnt. Many of the chains were torn off (one was given to a small girl as a lead for her dog) and the books remained neglected until Canon Streeter organised the rebuilding of the original presses in this century. The library has now been restored to its original splendour. Moreover, Hereford has yet another chained library in All Saints, a spacious church with a cool mediaeval atmosphere.

The chained libraries are a fitting memorial of a century in the city's history when it was a centre of intellectual excellence over a wide area. In the twelfth century men like Giraldus, Geoffrey of Monmouth and Walter Map were in close contact with bishops of the calibre of Robert of Bethune, Gilbert Foliot and Robert of Melun, with local poets like Hue de Rotelande and Simon de Freine, and with scientists like Roger Puer. "Come with honour to our City", wrote Simon de Freine to Giraldus "you will be happy at Hereford, the true home of the Seven Arts". The presence in the chained library of no fewer than 92 volumes of twelfth century manuscripts, many of superb quality, gives substance to his claim.

But as well as being intellectually eminent in the middle ages, Hereford has produced notable artists in later centuries. Thomas Traherne was the son of a local shoemaker. David Garrick was born here, as was Roger Kemble, the father of Sarah Siddons. Nell Gwynne was a Hereford girl and her grandson was bishop when the Cathedral collapsed. David Cox was drawing master at the school and John Bull was the organist. John Davies and Richard Gething,

Broad Street and St Peter's Church, Hereford.   *Wyedean Tourist Board*

two of the greatest English calligraphers, worked here in the seventeenth century. And the city was one of the founders of the oldest of all musical festivals, The Three Choirs.

Elgar came to live here in 1904 and a year later composed The Introduction and Allegro for Strings. The inspiration came from a song he heard on the Wye, but he hoped that all the waters of Wye would not wash the Welsh blood out of its body, "the work is really a tribute to that sweet borderland where I have made my home". After composing the First Symphony, the Violin Concerto and patenting a process for making sulphuretted hydrogen, he moved to a large London house. But when someone observed that he must be living in clover, he replied "I don't know about the clover — I've left that behind at Hereford". He came back for the last time to conduct "The Dream of Gerontius" in the Cathedral in 1933, the year before he died.

Some of the old town walls remain, as does part of a Saxon rampart, while the great hall of the Bishop's Palace dates from the twelfth century. The Conningsby Hospital was built on the remains of a house of the Knights of St John of Jerusalem in 1614, to provide for "two of the most valuable characters in society (although generally the most neglected) the worn-out soldier and the superannuated faithful servant". The Cathedral School has been in existence since at least 1348, when Richard Cornewall was appointed "to rule and discipline it with birch and rod", and the College of Vicars Choral was founded in 1396.

The fifteenth century Booth Hall (now an hotel), the seventeenth century Old House (now a museum), the unique Blackfriars' Cross, Thomas Hardwick's Nelson column, the Catholic church of St Francis Xavier (in imitation of the Treasury of the Athenians at Delphi), Sir Robert Smirke's Shire Hall, the impressive frontage of the Green Dragon, and F. R. Kempson's extraordinary Gothic facade on the public library, with animals peering over the parapet, all add variety to the streets.

Hereford is, however, above all, a market town, and its superb triangular market place still provides its hub. Bernard Shaw reckoned that it was at least three glacial periods behind the other cities of England, and industry has certainly played little part in its development until this century. But back on the tree-lined river, to which Hereford so truly belongs, the nineteenth century saw a brief upsurge of activity, in the building of steam-ships.

The first was probably the *Paul Pry*, launched before 6,000 people in 1827. It was floated down to Chepstow for fitting but had to be submerged to pass under Wilton Bridge. Its life on the river was short in spite of cheap fares and plentiful refreshments. It was followed by the *Water Witch*, 80 foot long, and then, in 1902, by the *Wilton Castle*, a stern-wheel steamer, flat bottomed and designed to carry 100 passengers at just under 8 knots. It lasted barely ten years and was abandoned in 1912 for lack of trade.

It marked the end of the Wye Tour as a commercial enterprise. Nowadays nothing with a deeper draught than the canoe or the racing eight can use the river for any distance; and for long stretches the water remains untroubled except for the fishermen and the occasional heron.

Looking back towards Hereford, one can be thankful that it too has regained much of its early charm and tranquillity. It has escaped the brutal destruction that has accompanied the re-development of the other Three Choir cities, Worcester and Gloucester, and has retained a stable, unhurried, civilised core; and it is not difficult to see why Traherne, thinking back to his childhood and the wonder he felt on entering its streets, remembered them

"As burnish't and as new
As if before none ever did them view:
They seem'd to me
Environ'd with Eternity."

Advertising the Wye Tour in 1892. From Stooke's Map of the River Wye.

ARCHENFIELD

R. LUGG

HEREFORD

- HAMPTON BISHOP
- MORDIFORD
- EVEN PITTS
HOLME LACY •
- FOWNHOPE
- CAPLAR CAMP
BALLINGHAM • • BROCKHAMPTON
CAREY •
- HOW CAPLE
HOARWITHY • FAWLEY •
KINGS FOY • • HOLE IN THE WALL
CAPLE • STRANGFORD
SELLACK • •

R. GARRON

BRIDSTOW •
WILTON • ○ ROSS

- WALFORD
GOODRICH • • KERNE BRIDGE
WELSH
BICKNOR •
WHITCHURCH • • LYDBROOK
DOWARD • • ENGLISH BICKNOR
SYMONDS YAT • • COLDWELL ROCKS

HEREFORD TO SYMONDS YAT

CHAPTER FOUR

Hereford to Ross

THE river between Hereford and Ross is less noted for its scenery than the more widely advertised Lower Wye. It has even, unjustly, been described as insipid. But it contains more interesting churches than any other stretch except that between Hay and Hereford; and in Holme Lacy, How Caple, Hoarwithy and Brockhampton, a wider range of architectural style than can be found over any similar distance.

Soon after leaving Hereford, the river passes Dinedor Hill with its iron-age fort on the right and **Hampton Bishop** on the left. Its fine Norman church is remarkable for its three reredoses: a noble, damaged stone one in the side chapel; another, given with a barrel organ in 1823, misplaced behind the font; and a third, presented by the bishop in 1912, at the east end behind the altar.

After three changes of direction, the river flows north to **Mordiford**, where it is joined by "that more lovely Lugg" as Drayton called it:

"For Hereford, although her Wye she hold so dear

Yet Lugg (whose longer course doth grace the goodly Sheere,

And with his plenteous stream so many brooks doth bring)

Of all hers that be North is absolutely King."

Mordiford church, the bridge, and the palatial rectory make a pleasing group. The rectory, which looks as if it cost twice as much as the other two together, is a monument to clerical affluence and good taste. The church, to some extent the victim of circumstance, was deformed in the early nineteenth century when the central tower was demolished and the present one, with its pyramid roof, was built at the south-west end.

Until 1811, the tower was adorned with a painting of a fine green dragon, four yards long, and inscribed underneath:

"This is the true effigy of the strange

Prodigious monster, which our wood did range.

In Eastwood it by Garson's hand was slayne,

A truth which old mythologists maintayne."

The Mordiford dragon may possibly have originated as the wyvern of St Guthlac's Priory, but "old mythologists" and others maintained that it persecuted the village from Serpent Lane ("the grass never grew there") until it was finally disposed of by a public-spirited condemned prisoner called Garson. He hid in a cider barrel and shot it with an arrow fired through the bung-hole.

Unfortunately for the hero, the dragon's dying breath set fire to the barrel and he died with his victim.

Inside the church is a wall monument to Margaret Brydges. She was a Vaughan from Courtfield (further down river) and, in 1655, died at her prayers "in the forme as you see her portrature". There is a pleasing tablet to James Hereford by Peter Hollins, and occasional dragons in the window-glass and on the backs of the chairs.

Mordiford's floods came mainly from the Lugg which enters the Wye at an awkward angle. There is a tablet in the chancel recording one, in 1811, when the village was visited by a great storm "which produced a wall of water twenty feet deep", destroying a barn, a cider mill and many gardens, and drowning four people. The bridge survived. It is one of the older Herefordshire bridges, being partly fourteenth and partly sixteenth century.

The Wye is then turned by the rocks of the Woolhope Dome south towards **Holme Lacy**. The road crosses Even Pit bridge to reach it, and it was here that the largest Wye salmon was found in 1920. It was dead, and the man who found it measured it as 59½ inches long and 33½ inches in girth. It was by no means the largest fish caught in the river. That honour probably belongs to the sturgeon which was seen near Breinton in 1846. The man who saw it, stripped, flung himself into the water, and attacked it with a knife. When he eventually got it ashore it was found to weigh 162 lbs. and was 8 foot 6 inches long. Another sturgeon, caught near Hoarwithy, weighed 137 lbs.

Holme Lacy House, the largest in the county, is now a hospital. It was built for the second Viscount Scudamore in c. 1680 and had superb overmantels, probably by Grinling Gibbons, which have been dispersed; and magnificent plaster ceilings, which remain. His father, "the good Lord Scudamore", was a confirmed royalist, a diplomat and a scholar, the friend of Milton, Laud, Grotius and Hobbes, and the restorer of the great Cistercian abbey at Dore in the Golden Valley. He also gave the county its most famous cider apple, the Red Streak, extolled by Phillips in his poem on cider:

"Let every tree in every garden own
The Red Streak as supreme, whose pulpous fruit
With gold irradiate and vermillion shines."

Before the century was out, it was being planted in the American colonies and, once Andrew Yarranton had developed the process of bottling cider, the Duke of Chandos was sending to his picture dealer in Italy "40 dozen Herefordshire Redstreak cider".

The Scudamores lived like Renaissance princes at Holme Lacy and the first Viscount's immaculate accounts show him, in 1632 for instance, spending over £76 on apparel, £68 on his water works, over £57 on a four-day journey to London, £6: 4: 0 on physick, and 6/8 on his losses at shuffleboard.

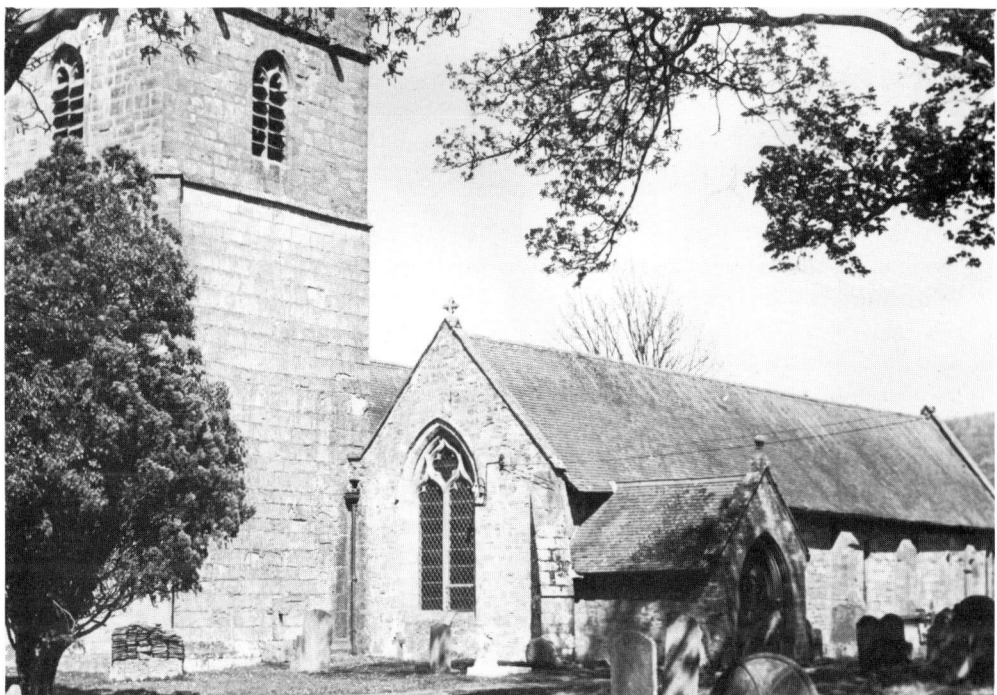

Holme Lacy. *The Author*

Well away from the house, standing on the edge of the water meadows, in a churchyard ringed with fine trees, is the church of St Cuthbert. The main body of the building is equally divided between nave and south aisle, while the chancel and south chapel are also the same size, an arrangement which the Royal Commission on Historical Monuments calls "not without architectural interest". It is spacious and light; there are plain seventeenth century benches; a fine gilt wooden eagle lectern; and some elegant Scudamore tombs. One of these, from the early eighteenth century, is exuberantly ornate and shows James Scudamore, reclining Roman fashion in Roman fancy dress, waiting expectantly for two cherubs appearing from behind the stage curtains to crown him with a large wreath.

Next to the church, and almost over-topping it, is the imposingly erect seventeenth century vicarage. It stands on a terrace and rises to three storeys, as if reaching out of the floods. Near it was one of the largest of all pear trees which, according to an 1870 guide book, had covered, by layering, a quarter of an acre, and gave from twelve to sixteen hogsheads of perry for many years.

The river continues to meander through broad fields to **Fownhope**, a village which depended on the barge traffic for much of its trade. Boats carried bark downstream and returned with coal from Lydbrook, while pleasure boats took travellers to Ross, Monmouth and Chepstow. The dangers of this deceptively placid river were shown in 1819 when a coal barge, with 25 tons on board, capsized just off the village and the crew of three were drowned.

As late as 1905, men were still toying with the idea of making the Wye navigable, and one of the more bizarre schemes involved a collapsible weir at Fownhope, twenty feet high, but with winches and rollers for drawing boats over the sides. The aim was to raise the level of the river above it by 4½ feet, and so allow steamboats to operate between Belmont and Fownhope. The project was abandoned in view of the concerted objections of the salmon fishermen.

The large church, with its Norman central tower and shingle spire, has a splendid Romanesque tympanum preserved in the west wall. It shows the Virgin and Child guarded by a ferocious lion of St Mark, with the usual enormous claws, and a mild eagle of St John, looking more like a parrot than a bird of prey. The whole composition is typical of the twelfth century school of Herefordshire sculpture, with beautiful "damp fold" treatment of the clothing, falling in graceful pleats from the Virgin's knees.

There is also a large fourteenth century chest, two fonts, one seventeenth and the other eighteenth century, and Leonardo's Last Supper, done in needlework by a Victorian vicar. The village has the remains of its stocks, a *Green Man* pub, and a milestone showing that Hereford is 6¼ miles and 56 yards away.

After Fownhope the river changes direction twice, passing under Caplar Hill with its large oval hill fort which descends almost sheer to the river. Beyond it is **Brockhampton**, high on the left bank. Here in 1901 W. R. Lethaby replaced the ruined Holy Trinity with his ingenious Arts and Crafts All Saints as a memorial to the parents of Alice Foster. The vaulting of the

Herefordshire from Caplar Camp. *Monmouth Museum*

Brockhampton-by-Ross, 1901-2.   *The Author*

chancel is concrete and the roof is thatched, as is the lych-gate. There is a Morris tapestry designed by Burne-Jones and choir stalls carved with local wild flowers. The flowers are repeated on the altar frontal and on the 72 linen prayer book covers "left on the altar by an anonymous donor". It is very much a family church, the alms-box being paid for with money found on one of the sons in the Grenadier Guards who was mortally wounded at Neuve Chapelle in 1915. It is well worth leaving the Wye to visit this unique church.

Across the river is **Ballingham**, with its church dedicated to St Dubricius, the evangelist of Archenfield. It stands amongst farm buildings on a ridge overlooking the deep valley, and is mercilessly restored and locked. There is a classical Scudamore monument of 1649 inside, and a nice eighteenth century sundial outside, incongruously set on the steps of the churchyard cross.

There was a forge on the river here, erected by Lord Scudamore in 1628, making iron for export by barge to Bristol. Some of the accounts have survived and show that the bargemen were liable to "cocket money", or tolls to the King, the Earl of Worcester and the "cyty of Monmouth".

Ballingham is one of the eastern boundaries of **Archenfield**, the old Welsh kingdom of Erging, which was roughly enclosed by the Wye from Ballingham to Monmouth, and by the Monnow from Monmouth to Pontrilas. Apart from being one of the cradles of Celtic christianity, there is some evidence that in the tenth century the inhabitants were the Dunsaete, a mixed community with a long-established tradition of Anglo-Welsh co-operation. It has been suggested by Sir Frank Stenton that this may account for the absence of Offa's Dyke in their territory.

The prosaic, and usually accepted, derivation of the name is from Ariconium, a Roman settlement near Ross but outside the boundary. Leland, more poetically, thought it came from The Field of Erinacius. Equally ingenious, and even more unlikely, was the theory that it came from Urchinfield, the field of hedgehogs.

When the Normans reached Hereford they overran Archenfield, but continued the pre-Conquest practice of allowing the inhabitants to retain their Celtic customs in return for military service, as vanguard on any advance into Wales and as rearguard on the way out. The customs which they retained are set out in Domesday Book and include freedom from most customary dues, and the right to wage private war: "If so be that a Welshman shall kill a Welshman, the relatives of the slain meet together and plunder the slayer and his kin, and burn their houses until on the morrow at about noon the corpse is buried. Of the plunder the king has a third part but they have all the rest without hindrance".

Long after Welshmen further west had lost their independence, the men of Archenfield were enjoying their traditional way of life. In the thirteenth century they owed no services at all except a payment of 19 marks and the service of 50 men for 15 days against Wales and for one day against England.

The road from Ballingham runs down from the escarpment to the river and then along the tree-lined banks to **Hoarwithy**. The Wye, meandering through rich pasture, here provides some of the best salmon fishing in Herefordshire, and this embittered a famous legal battle at the beginning of the century.

The landholders whose property adjoined the river, the "brinkers", had always claimed the right to fish in the "free waters" between Holme Lacy and Strangford, near Foy, provided that the fish they caught were exposed for sale at the fish board in Hoarwithy. In 1907, the Earl of Chesterfield from Holme Lacy brought an action against two men for fishing in the free water from boats. The case was first decided for the boatmen, reversed by the Court of Appeal in 1908, and then, in 1911, decided for the earl in the House of Lords by one vote.

Hoarwithy has, in St Catherine's, one of the most surprising churches in Herefordshire. It is reached by an imposing flight of steps, which leads beneath a campanile into a cloister walk before reaching the south door. It was designed by J. P. Seddon in the 1880s for the Reverend William Poole, who had been vicar there for nearly forty-six years. No expense was spared on a splendid Byzantine east end with a Pantokrator in gold mosaic in the apse. There are marble columns, cosmati work, fine window glass, and elaborate

Romanesque-revival capitals. The stalls, said to have been made from the vicar's own oaks, are carved with local saints and scenes from the life of St Dubricius. The church stands above the pleasant village in the way that similar churches surmount the hill towns of Southern Italy.

The iron bridge at Hoarwithy leads across the river to **King's Caple**, where the church dominates the peninsula formed by the horse-shoe bend of the Wye. Its red sandstone spire, protective yews, and the ramparts of Caple Tump, can be seen for many miles and from all directions.

It is a spacious church with a side chapel thronged with the tombs of the owners of Aramstone, a house which has been demolished. The monuments range from the pompous extravagance of "the last of ye Marretts of Aramstone whose settlement there (as it appears in Deeds) was earlier than ye 10th of Hen 6", to a charming relief by Flaxman (1814) of a young widower gazing at his small child. There is an accompanying memorial by Westmacott to the child's grandmother. A simple tablet to John Roberts states movingly that, in 1806, he "Exchanged Time for Eternity".

There are original seventeenth century pews, a scraped font, as at Dixton, a Jacobean pulpit with tester, and on the benefaction board in the gallery, a Scudamore bequest of "Cake money so-called". King's Caple is one of three churches, Sellack and Hentland are the others, where Pax cakes are distributed on Palm Sunday with the ancient greeting "Peace and Good Neighbourhood".

Back on the right bank, with a taller spire, is **Sellack** church, isolated in its valley, and with a rare dedication to St Tyssilio. It contains some effusive memorials, including one to a doctor, "the author of many laborious works on medicine, insanity and language", a fine Jacobean pulpit with tester, and an east window inscribed "R S 1630" (possibly Rowland Scudamore) but containing earlier glass. There is also a mediaeval chest, with diagrams on the lid

How Caple Church.   *The Author*

Royal Arms of William III at
How Caple.   *The Author*

which are thought to have been used when playing Nine Men's Morris. In the
churchyard are some noble yews, complete quiet, and a view, across the water
meadows, of a dreadful housing estate at King's Caple.

The village was originally Baysham, and Leland refers to "Beysham alias
Cellack". It had an important ford where one of John Kyrle's descendants, who
had survived service in India, the Walcheren expedition and the Peninsular
War, was drowned in 1819. A bridge was built near the ford in 1895, "To the
Honour of God and the Lasting Union of these Parishes for the use of all". It
was to be maintained by the vicar.

The Reverend Augustine Ley, vicar when the bridge was built, was a
great botanist, who published many valuable papers on local wild flowers, and
took a leading part in the production of *The Flora of Herefordshire* in 1889.

The river now runs north-east past **Fawley**, a fine group of farm
buildings, surrounding a chapel. Very small, it contains an unusual, but
pleasing, triple chancel arch and a tub-shaped font.

Beyond it, on the same side and just before the river changes direction
again, is **How Caple**. Hidden amongst the trees, and overshadowed by the
neighbouring great house, is a splendid church, rebuilt by the Gregorys in
1693. There is a Jacobean pulpit, with a tester copied from Oxford Cathedral,
and a corkscrew screen supporting a superb royal arms of William III in gilded
cedarwood. The reredos has a carefully carved model of the Last Supper, and in
the Gregory chapel there is a sixteenth century German altarpiece. There are
also several large wall monuments, one of the largest to the Reverend Edward
Stillingfleet who died in 1795, "no less respected for his private virtue than his
honourable descent". He was rector for only twenty days. The font is
mediaeval and was found beneath one, with acanthus leaves and the date of
1698, which now stands in the churchyard.

One of the seventeen miracles accredited to St Thomas of Hereford by the
Papal Commissioners in 1307 involved Nicholas Fisher, a boy from How
Caple, who was drowned here on 28th May, 1300. He had been looking for
something in his father's boat which was moored to the bank, when he slipped

and fell into the river. The accident was seen by Margaret Francis from the other bank but no one heard her screams and the boy lay in the water until his father found him. He was lifted out with his teeth clenched, "livid like lead", and placed in a warm bed. There the rigid body was "measured" with thread which would form the wick and determine the length of the candle to offer to St Thomas. He recovered within a few hours and on the following Tuesday his parents and many villagers walked to Hereford to report the miracle to the Cathedral canons.

An iron foot-bridge leads across the river onto the fields in front of **Foy** church at Hole-in-the-Wall (a name derived from a nineteenth century pot-house). The Wye is wide with occasional shallows, and the church stands on a platform above the flood plain. Alongside, amongst splendid trees, is the eighteenth century vicarage, recently up-graded to Foy Hall.

St Mary's is very much the shrine of the Abrahall family whose fine, freshly-coloured memorials adorn the chancel walls with portrait busts, heraldry, skulls and hedgehogs. The hedgehogs, which recur on a boss under the screen, are part of the Abrahall arms. The east window is an almost exact replica of the one at Sellack and was put up in 1640 on the orders of John Abrahall. There is a good fourteenth century south door, a dug-out chest, a Jacobean pulpit, and in a recess, a very small effigy of a thirteenth century woman, in a long pleated dress, her feet resting on an unpleasant mask.

The place has a timeless quality which is exemplified by the remarkable fact that two vicars, between them, spanned one hundred and seven years, from 1816 to 1923.

The countryside around Foy is a maze of quiet lanes, the river valley widening towards **Ross** after rounding the hill on which Brampton Abbotts stands. The Hereford railway crossed the Wye at Backney Bridge and then accompanied it towards the town. Camden found that Ross was noted for smiths, and Defoe called it "a good old town, famous for good cider, a great manufacture of iron ware and a good trade on the River Wye, and nothing else as I remember except it was a monstrous fat woman they would have me go to see".

The approach from the river is disappointing, marred by a depressing housing estate and a skeletal electricity station on the left, and the thunder of the traffic on the A 40 ahead. But once under the fine new bridge, the town rises above the horse-shoe bend of the river in terraces on which John Kyrle's eighteenth century town planning is pleasantly mingled with mock-mediaeval battlements and the imposing facade of the British and Foreign School of c. 1837. There is a discreet car park, a municipal shrubbery, the inevitable charitable wishing well, and a popular meadow between the river and the town. The whole scene is dominated by the splendid spire of the parish church, rising against the background of Penyard Hill.

St Mary's Church, Ross. The pinnacles being repaired.   *The Author*

Hoarwithy Church, c. 1885.   *The Author*

The spire was rebuilt in 1721 by Nathaniel Wilkinson and it surmounts a spacious church with graceful thirteenth century nave arcades. There is a fine thirteenth century east window and a splendid collection of tombs. The most surprising of these is that of Colonel William Rudhall. He stands erect, grasping his iron sword, dressed in extraordinary theatrical trappings as if about to take the lead in a Roman television epic. He died in 1651 and surveys from on high other members of his family, lying more tranquilly at his feet.

They include the alabaster effigies of Henry VII's attorney-general, reposing with his wife on a tomb chest. It is adorned with many saints, ranging from Edward the Confessor to St Zita, the patron of housemaids, holding her flowering loaf. Like Alfred, she was left in charge of the cooking, but told her beads instead. Unlike Alfred, her loaves flowered instead of burning.

Other memorials include an impressive tomb chest to John Rudhall, holding his wife's hand (1636); and a wall monument of almost the same date to Nathaniel Hill, kneeling at his prayers. In the chancel is a simple brass plate to a local mercer who died in 1622. It includes the whole of Sir Walter Raleigh's great poem *The Conclusion*, finished the night before his execution and copied into his bible:

"Even such is time which takes in trust
Our youth and joies and all we have . . . "

The inscription ends with a line from Virgil, "Vivat post funera virtus". Raleigh died in 1618; the lettering of the tablet is consistent with 1622; but the first known printed copy of the poem is 1628. How did a Ross mercer's family obtain a manuscript copy so soon after his death? Was it through the Rudhalls with their court connections? This small brass is one of the most interesting in the church. And much more agreeable than the tablet to a former curate, who died in 1854:

"God only knows who next shall follow me:
Reader Prepare! Perhaps it may be thee."

The town itself, with its pleasant seventeenth century market hall, its Prospect, its almshouses, its Georgian hotels and winding streets, owes much to John Kyrle, "The Man of Ross", who lived from 1637 to 1724, and who has since suffered from much indifferent verse:

"Whose Causeway parts the vale with shady rows?
Whose seats the weary traveller repose?
Who taught the heav'n directed spire to rise?
'The Man of Ross' each lisping babe replies."

In fact, the lisping babes soon forgot their benefactor and Pope, who wrote his eulogy at Holme Lacy, was surprised to find that, seven years after Kyrle's death, there was no memorial to him:

"And what? No monument, inscription, stone?
His race, his name, his form almost unknown?"

73

Pope used Kyrle's self-effacing generosity as an example of the way in which limited wealth could best be used.

But it was not until 1776, more than fifty years after he died, that the huge monument, with his portrait by Marsh of Ross, was placed in the church. And when Charles Heath wrote his description of the town in 1799 he noted that almost all Kyrle's benefactions had been vandalised; his seats on the Prospect destroyed by "loose and idle people"; his water-supply out of order and the fountain full of dead animals; his summer-house uncared for and its Latin inscription defaced; his garden turned into a bowling green and his elms felled by successive incumbents in search of firewood. It is said that the climbing plants now inside the church are meant to commemorate the tree which is reputed to have appeared there when one of these clerical vandals cut down the last of his elms.

A less well-known contemporary of Kyrle was the rector of Ross, John Newton D.D., a notable astronomer and mathematician and an early advocate of the reform of the grammar schools by broadening the curriculum. He was the author of many books, including "The Scale of Interest or The Use of Decimal Fractions and Table of Logarithms composed and published for the use of a Mathematical and Grammar School to be set up at Ross. 1688". There is a long Latin memorial to him in the sanctuary of the parish church.

By the end of the eighteenth century, Ross had established itself as the headquarters of the Wye Tour. John Egerton, who had been collated to the rectory of Ross by his father, the bishop of Hereford in 1745, built the first Wye pleasure boat, on which he took his guests up and down the river. When Gilpin had decided that the Wye provided the finest opportunities for the man of taste to view the picturesque, boats and boatmen multiplied. Eventually it became so commercialised that many travellers preferred to walk or ride.

There was a further decline when the exile of Napoleon made continental travel less of a risk to the timid, and although the vicar of Walford thought the decline was due to lack of enterprise on the part of the people of Ross, nothing came of his remedies. He suggested that what Ross needed was better lodging houses, more billiard tables, "a public gaudy galley", and a system by which travellers were returned to Ross the moment they set foot in Chepstow. Lack of commercial-mindedness always pleased Cobbett, and when he was here in 1821, Ross was one of the few towns in the West which gained his approval. There was nothing of either finery or misery, "it is a good plain country town or settlement of tradesmen whose business is that of supplying the cultivators of the soil. It presents nothing of rascality and roguishness of look which you see on almost every visage in the borough towns".

When the tour was at its height, travellers were escorted to their boats by the owners so that "their ears should not be pained with a coarseness of language, too frequently heard from the navigators of public rivers". Once launched, there was no such control, although the *Hope and Anchor* Inn prided itself on providing "good boats *and* civil men".

Leaving the Dock Pitch, the craft passed Wilton Castle, which had been destroyed in the Civil War, and under Wilton Bridge. It had been built in 1597, to replace a wooden one, and contains on the parapet an early eighteenth century sundial with the words:

"Esteem thy precious time
Which pass so swift away.
Prepare thee for eternity
And do not make delay."

It is said that, during the great plague in Ross in 1637, the angles of the bridge were used for the sale of farm produce, money being thrown into a bucket before being picked up. The death pits are marked in the churchyard by a cross with the words: "Plague Anno Dom. 1637. Burials 315. Libera nos Domine". Ross was so destitute after this catastrophe that a county rate of £55 a week was collected for several months to provide for the survivors.

Ross. *The Author*

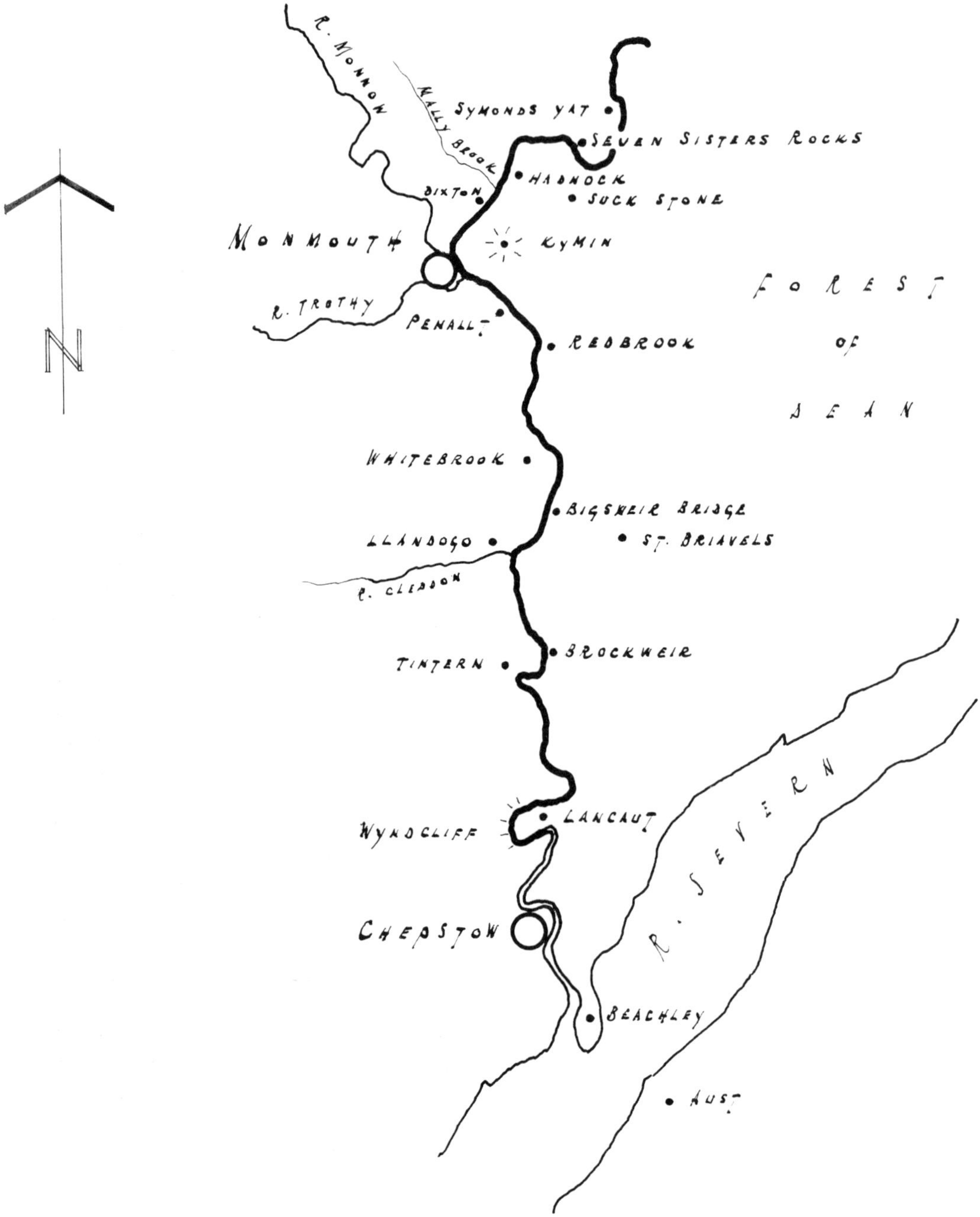

N

R. MONNOW

NALLY BROOK

SYMONDS YAT

SEVEN SISTERS ROCKS

DIXTON

HADNOCK

SUCK STONE

MONMOUTH

KYMIN

FOREST

R. TROTHY

PENALL·

REDBROOK

OF

DEAN

WHITEBROOK

BIGSWEIR BRIDGE

LLANDOGO

ST. BRIAVELS

R. CLEDDON

TINTERN

BROCKWEIR

R. SEVERN

WYNDCLIFF

LANCAUT

CHEPSTOW

BEACHLEY

AUST

SYMONDS YAT TO CHEPSTOW

CHAPTER FIVE

Ross to Monmouth

B EYOND Wilton Bridge the river runs through a flood plain of flat meadows, many of them now denuded of their once fine elms through disease. Gilpin thought this stretch of the river "tame", his favourite epithet for anything not correctly picturesque. But Cobbett, looking down on the valley from Penyard Hill, wrote, "There wants nothing but the Autumnal colours of the American trees to make this the most beautiful spot I ever beheld".

Pylons now disfigure the landscape, though the lines have been put underground in front of Goodrich Castle. This was due to a public enquiry at which the Electricity Board claimed that to do so would cost one million pounds more per mile. They may well have lost their case because they were then unable to answer the question, "More than what?"

On the left bank, across the fields and over the disused railway embankment, is **Walford**. The church looks curiously naked since its spire was destroyed by lightning in 1813 and since, more recently, the gravestones were placed with their backs to the churchyard walls, as if facing a firing squad. It contains a largely thirteenth century interior, a pleasant north arcade, a seventeenth century funeral helm over the chancel arch, several hatchments and a variety of wall monuments. There is a graceful early eighteenth century memorial to the Stratford family, and a simpler one to Eusebius Beeston, drowned in the Wye in 1815, at the age of twenty-six. The Reverend T. D. Fosbrook, a former vicar, is commemorated as "a scholar, and antiquary and local historian. To posterity he has bequeathed the labours of an indefatigable industry" (to wit *British Monacism*, 2 volumes, *The Encyclopaedia of Antiquities*, 2 volumes, and many other works). He is best remembered for his book on the Wye, published in 1811. It is one of the few written at that time with first-hand local knowledge and Wordsworth had a copy of it in his library at Rydal when he died.

The parish contains several good houses, notably Hill Court, early eighteenth century with Adam embellishments inside and fine gates outside; and Upper Wythall, a noble sixteenth century timber-framed farmhouse. As in so many Wye villages there is also a lot of modern in-filling. Back on the Wye, towards Goodrich, is the Dog Hole, a salmon pool made famous by Robert Pashley, one of the great local fishermen.

Walford means "the Welsh ford" and takes its name from the Roman crossing here. In the late nineteenth century a hoard of 18,000 Roman coins of

Left, Funeral Helm, c. 1600 in Walford Church and *right*, St George and the dragon, c. 1150 at Ruardean Church.

Monmouth Museum and the Author

c. 350 A.D. was found in three urns not far from the church. Later, a ferry operated on the site of the ford, and it was here that the Wye tourists made their first stop and breakfasted. They then walked across the fields to **Goodrich Castle**, towering majestically over the river below. In those days it was romantically coated in ivy, and even more romantically described by its aged custodian. Today it has been shaved, mown, signposted and accurately described by the Department of the Environment; and is a fine example of a compact border castle, built from the rock of its huge dry moat, and with its keep, gatehouse and curtain wall almost intact.

Wordsworth is reputed to have met the little girl who became the subject of *We are seven* here in 1793. Nearly fifty years later he was enraged to see "a fantastic new castle set up on the same ridge as if to show how far modern art can go in surpassing all that could be done by antiquity and nature". He was referring to Goodrich Court, built by Edward Blore, to house a great collection of armour. It was one of the first houses to be opened free "to every respectable and well-clothed individual, who is", according to the guide book issued at the time, "allowed all the benefits of the inspection secured to the most high-minded stranger".

It stood on a platform, a short distance from the thirteenth century castle, and was demolished after the last war, just over a hundred years after Wordsworth had yearned "to blow away this impertinent structure".

78

The church, with a tall broach spire on an unbuttressed tower, is some way from the castle. It is a large building which, like many in Archenfield, belonged once to Monmouth Priory. The painter Joshua Cristall and his wife are buried in the churchyard, which was once ringed by Redstreak apple trees. There is a pleasant seat, facing towards the river, and a tombstone which commemorates "the two beloved wives of John Rogers". Hannah died on the 12th of November 1837, and Marylyn on the 17th of July 1838.

The communion cup, dated 1617, was given to the parish by Dean Swift in memory of his grandfather, Thomas Swift, who was vicar here during the Civil War and who lies buried under the communion table. He had brought upon himself Parliamentary hostility by preaching a sermon in Ross on the text "Render unto Caesar the things that are Caesar's". But he practised what he preached and, in 1645, set out to render to the king at Raglan Castle the whole of the family fortune, consisting of 300 coins sewn into his waistcoat. Meanwhile his wife and ten children, destitute and starving, were ejected from the vicarage by the Parliamentary soldiers.

The old vicarage, now called New House Farm, is Y-shaped and was built by Thomas Swift, with his initials and the date, 1636, on the pillars of the porch. Goodrich has other attractive houses although, since it has become fashionable, there has been some expensive development west of the church. Down in the village is *Ye Olde Hostelrie*, built to match Blore's Goodrich Court and meant to represent the spirit of that place, while along the road to Kerne Bridge are the remains of Flanesford Priory.

This was a late Augustinian foundation in 1346, and only the refectory in the long barn and the fish pond are left. The castle and the priory were all that most of the Wye tourists had time to look at, and the time allowed depended on the weather. Gilpin endured torrential rain, but for Bloomfield, back on the boat, "in perfect beauty, perfect ease, The awning trembled in the breeze". They then passed the spot where Kerne Bridge now stands. It was not built, with its toll house, until 1828, the year in which the lower Wye was finally opened up with the building of the Monmouth to Chepstow Road.

The railway bridge, which follows Kerne Bridge, was built even later. It carried the Ross line over the river and under Coppet Hill, to join the Severn and Wye line at Lydbrook. Bishopswood, on the left bank, was once the terminus of the tramroad which preceded the railway. It had many iron forges and acquired its All Saints church in 1845.

The river now begins a long right-handed sweep through steeply rising hills, those on the right in Archenfield (with quarries which, according to Gilpin, provided the stone for Bristol Bridge) and those on the left in the equally independent **Forest of Dean**. It is curiously alien, "a little country on its own" of undulating woodland, uninspiring villages, industrial refuse and basic, down-to-earth place-names: The Scowles, The Pludds, The Hudnalls,

The Tufts, The Purlieu, The Slaughter, Knockalls, Wigpool, Nuppend, Slade Bottom, Mork, Stroat, Bunjups and (to prove the rule) Euroclydon.

It is an area which has been very much subject to its own laws, whether they were the harsh royal restrictions imposed in the interests of the deer, or the courts and privileges of the Free Miners which go back to the fourteenth century. Its natural resources have been ruthlessly exploited, whether it was timber for the navy, charcoal for the forges, or coal for domestic use.

The Romans plundered its iron ore, and the Scowles remain to mark their quarries. They built the first roads and left a temple to the Celtic god Nodens in Lydney Park. Saxon influence remains in a fine length of Offa's Dyke. The Normans introduced itinerant forges and their kings monopolised the hunting. The Free Miners were often used as engineers on military expeditions, and their supervision within the forest was in the hands of the Gaveller in the same way that the administration of the forest as a whole was the responsibility of the Constable of St Briavels and the Verderers.

The *Complete English Traveller*, in 1746, found that "coals are so cheap here, that 'tis common to see a good Fire in the Meanest Cottage: for a

The Wye from Goodrich Castle.   *The Author*

Horse-load costs but Two-pence at the Mouth of the Pit". Many of the free miners' pits have names of as home-spun a quality as their villages: Strip-and-at-it, Ready Penny, Luck-is-all, Near the Last, Prosper-on-Time, Pluck Penny, Young Men's Folly, The Stay-and-Drink, James's Folly and The Gentlemen Colliers.

In spite of industrial exploitation, the majesty of the forest remains, and there are villages, like Newland, Newnham and Staunton, of great charm. Systematic replanting by the Forestry Commission and successful resistance, so far, to the introduction of open-cast mining by the National Coal Board, have made it one of the most beautiful forests in the country. It is still the largest area in England where free grazing is available to people who are not landowners. And it has, still, a distinctive character and a flavour of independence which perpetuates its traditional past.

The fringes of the Forest contain many fine churches and it is worth going up the B 4227, just beyond Bishopswood, to visit one of them. **Ruardean** is a typical Forest village but the churchyard is superbly placed above the valley, with marvellous views over Herefordshire to the Black Mountains and Wales. It contains a vast number of finely carved tombstones, many of them marshalled around the walls as at Walford, others even more ruthlessly uprooted, truncated and then used as edging for the paths.

The slender fourteenth century spire has spectacular flying buttresses, and the ringing chamber, under the tower, is beautifully vaulted. There is a seventeenth century pulpit, some good coloured wall monuments, one in 1806 commemorating a "Sincere Friend and Benefactor of the Musical Society of this Church", and a rare Commonwealth font (1657). But the chief glory of the building is the Romanesque tympanum over the south door. It is the work of the Herefordshire school of craftsmen in c. 1150 and appears to be based on a carving of Constantine at Parthenay-le- Vieux. Here the sculptor has shown St George, his cloak flying in the wind, riding down the dragon and slaying it with his long lance.

Let into the wall of the lych-gate is a stone, given by the churchwardens in 1743, with a variation of the words on the sundial at Wilton Bridge:
"Redeeme thy precious Time
Which steals so fast away
And in Gods Hous forgiveness Ask
And for Salvation Pray."
Even the county boundaries here are unusual. Most of Coppet Hill and the land around Goodrich ferry, once part of the lordship of Monmouth, remained outliers of Monmouthshire until 1844.

From Kerne bridge, the Wye makes an almost complete eight mile circuit to arrive back within a mile of the bridge. In so doing it encircles Coppet Hill, a bare, bracken-covered expanse which contains **Courtfield**, once the home of the Vaughans, an old Catholic family. To the Georgian house and Victorian chapel, has been added a modern extension, looking like a motor way cafè, its acres of glass reflecting the morning sun. Henry of Monmouth is said to have been taken to Courtfield for the sake of his health when very young, but the nursery has gone, although two of the legendary cradles, in which he certainly did not sleep, have survived, one of c. 1450 in the London Museum, the other, much later, at Badminton.

The Vaughans provided the only two local Jacobites to fight at Culloden. Both survived, escaped to Spain, married, and settled abroad. One of their descendants, John Francis, had thirteen children, four of the girls becoming nuns and six of the eight sons priests. The most famous of them was Cardinal Vaughan, founder of the Mill Hill Fathers, who now own Courtfield.

Being outside Herefordshire, and part of a strongly recusant county like Monmouthshire, Coppet Hill was a useful Catholic refuge in the penal times. This is commemorated by the fine wooden carving of a priest kneeling at prayer, which is said to have been carved by a fugitive hiding near the house. It is known as the Luck of Courtfield.

The river curves on, through steeply wooded hills, to **Lydbrook**, which Mr and Mrs Hall, writing in 1861, likened to Sheffield, "a busy bustling scene, smoke from the tall chimneys, boats and tramways taking coal and iron to Hereford and Monmouth". Lydbrook is still industrial though it now takes little notice of its river. A large housing estate, the Temco factory and Reed's Paper Works, with its gaunt central tower, dwarf the small Victorian church of **Welsh Bicknor** across the river.

This church, with its ornate spire, timber lych-gate and large churchyard cross, contains a fine thirteenth century effigy of a lady, flat and boneless, holding the folds of her long dress in one hand and a ribbon in the other, her head on a cushion and her feet on a small animal. The original Celtic foundation, Llangystennin, was dedicated to Constantine, one of the sons of Magnus Maximus, the Welsh Maxen Wledig, and Helena. The present church, re-dedicated to St Margaret, was built in 1858, and is overlooked by the enormous rectory, now a Youth Hostel, which Mr and Mrs Hall found "happy in the suggestions of the tranquil life which country clergymen, above all other men, enjoy".

Across the river, on the Gloucestershire side, the sister church of **English Bicknor** is surrounded by the massive ramparts of the castle. It is impressively mediaeval, with beakheads over one of the arcade arches, fourteenth century effigies, a royal arms of George III, and massed cherubs on the gravestones which pack the churchyard in the outer bailey.

Once under the disused Lydbrook railway bridge and past ferocious notices saying "Keep off the Cribbs", pastoral peace returns to one of the most beautiful stretches of the Wye. Taylor, the Water Poet, in a notable

Himalayan Balsam and morning mist near Whitchurch.   *Wyedean Tourist Board*

understatement, remarked that "the Wye doth runne a little crooked from Lydbrook". In fact, after making a circuit of Coppet Hill, it changes course completely to encircle Huntsham.

It was below Lydbrook, in the shadow of the splendid **Coldwell Rocks** (individually named after members of the Oxford Circuit, who caroused here on their way to Monmouth Assizes) that the Wye tourists had their second meal:

"Noon scorched the fields, the boat lay to,
The dripping oars had naught to do . . .
Here in one gay according mind
Upon the tranquil stream we din'd
As shepherds free on mountain heath,
Free as the fish that watch'd beneath
For falling crumbs where cooling lay
The wine that cheer'd us on our way."

Bloomfield was lucky in the weather on his tour and one of the rocks is named after him. Less fortunate was John Warre, aged sixteen, who, in 1804, unwisely went for a swim too soon after the meal, got cramp, and was drowned. His memorial is a large stone on the right bank, with a long inscription beginning "God's will be done" and ending with instructions, for anyone in similar difficulties, that "apparatus and directions for their application by the Humane Society, for the saving of persons apparently drowned, are lodged at the church of Coldwell". The only trouble with this well-meaning but permanently misleading statement is that there is not, nor has there ever been, a church at Coldwell.

When the boat reached the eastern side of **Symonds Yat**, the travellers disembarked and made their way up the winding path to the cottage of a guide where they were refreshed with cider. They were then escorted to the view point and shown the spires of Ross and Goodrich, the winding river, Archenfield and in the distance, the Black Mountains, the Malverns, and the Long Mynd. After standing on the iron-age camp and looking downstream to the Seven Sisters Rocks, they descended to rejoin their boat which, having travelled for four miles round the Huntsham peninsula, was back within half a mile of where they had disembarked.

The boat had passed the tributary Garron, with its forge, and out in the fields opposite, the Queen Stone, a large grooved monolith which was a great subject of speculation for nineteenth century antiquarians. It lies in the meadow below Huntsham Court, a seventeenth century house near a Roman settlement and a lost mediaeval chapel.

Across the river is **Whitchurch**, a village which has been transfixed by the A 40 and almost obliterated by a maze of fly-overs and roundabouts. Old Court, a fine sixteenth century mansion, has been disfigured by neon lights, and The Grange, a house where the painter Wilson Steer once lived, has been demolished. But the history of local agriculture has been splendidly displayed in the barn of Brook House which now houses one of the best private rural crafts museums in the country.

The church, dedicated to St Dubricius, is close to the riverside and has been subject to flooding. It has been heavily restored, but there is a good roof, a Norman font, and the pews are still numbered. In the porch is a memorial,

The view from Symonds Yat. *The Author*

with a long Latin inscription, to a seventeenth century vicar's wife: "Hic (juxta maritum) Requiescat Ann Betham . . . " and in the churchyard the graves of two more victims of the Wye.

The Ballinger brothers were drowned in 1853. The elder, aged seventeen:
"Sunk to rise no more in that swift stream;
Short was his life and all his hopes a dream."
And the younger, aged nine:
"The cruel waves ran over me
It was God's will it so should be."
There is a large churchyard cross, dated 1698, and a rather impressive Gwillim mausoleum. The coat-of-arms is dated 1744, but it is all in a sad state of disrepair, in spite of a large marble tablet in the church bequeathing money for its maintenance.

The church is, mercifully, screened by trees from the caravans, tents, coaches, boats and cafeterias which indulge the visitors to Symonds Yat. Wordsworth, who could not stand "improvers" and loathed white-washed houses and unnatural trees, would find little pleasure in this over-publicised beauty spot today. But the view from the Rock, in spite of all the twentieth century aids to sightseeing, remains one of the unspoilt wonders of Herefordshire, especially in spring or late autumn.

The Wye tourists rejoined their boats near the ferry and entered upon what Gilpin considered the most picturesque stretch of the whole river: steep wooded hills on either side, the rushing stream, the coracle fishermen, and above all the thunder of the iron forge, belching smoke and flames over the waters of **New Weir**. It belonged to the Duke of Kent and, because it remained in existence longer than any other weir, was hated by the fishermen higher up. To appease them, the duke offered to reduce the number of puncheons from twenty to two, but this was declared to be meaningless as it was argued that two would trap as many fish as twenty.

But the tourists were concerned only with the picturesque and here the sublime, the beautiful, the awful and the ridiculous came together in sketch-book, poetry and prose. Gilpin set the tone: "All was agitation and uproar; and every steep and every rock stared with wildness and terror". He saw nothing incongruous in smoke and industrial noise, provided it obeyed the rules of the picturesque. Wheatley thought that a scene "truly great and awful" was enhanced by the operation of engines; and Shaw agreed:
"All is hushed
Save ever and anon the thund'ring stroke
That beats the fiery mass, while upwards rise
The smoaky volumes sparkling through the air . . . "
This length of the river, especially below New Weir, was popular with the coracle fishermen. Large cork bungs were attached to the butts of their rods,

Near Hadnock.

Monmouth Museum

and when a fish was hooked, the rod was thrown into the water, and the boatman paddled after it until the fish had played itself out. It is still a fine fishing stretch, the pools between Lydbrook and Redbrook commemorating places, people and events: The Monument, The Lime Kiln, The Plum Tree, The Hospital, The Engine House, The Slaughter, The Bibblins, The Sliding Ground, Martin's Hole, John's Hole, Boyd's Rocks, Monmouth Bridge, Livox, The Halfway House, Bull's Back, Colman and The Warehouse (Redbrook).

Returning to New Weir, there is a footbridge across the river, an adventure centre at the Bibblins, a nature trail arranged by the Forestry Commission, and a landing-stage from which rafts of logs were launched to be floated down to Monmouth. They were felled some months after being stripped of their bark for the tanneries, the naked trees being left to die during the summer. Bloomfield noticed "the dark brown saplings flay'd alive" when he passed the Seven Sisters Rocks. Although it must have been a depressing sight, it is rarely commented on by the writers on the picturesque.

The Seven Sisters, limestone pinnacles on the right bank, have been undercut, probably by water when, two million years ago, the sea level was 600 feet higher, and the river washed the entrance to King Arthur's Cave on the Great Doward. The floor of this cave was excavated with dynamite in 1870, and the shattered bones of mammoth, hyena, woolly rhinoceros, cave bear and beaver are now in the Hereford and Monmouth museums. A less violent excavation in 1924 produced more of such material from what was once a hyena den, used for temporary shelter by Palaeolithic hunters.

On top of the neighbouring Little Doward is an iron-age hill fort with multiple ramparts and several tumuli. Until 1920 the summit was also adorned with a large iron observation tower, erected in the nineteenth century by the owner of Wyaston Leys. This house, enlarged by William Burn in 1861, is superbly placed above the valley. It looks across the river to the Forest of Dean and four famous stones: The Buckstone at Staunton, The Suckstone (estimated to weigh 4000 tons), The Near Harkening and The Far Harkening Rocks, said to have been used by the keepers to listen for poachers.

The whole limestone outcrop, The Great Doward on the right and Lady Park Wood on the left, is noted for its rare flora. On the former can be seen Autumn Gentian, Mountain St John's Wort, Horseshoe Vetch, Pencilled Cranesbill and many orchids. Across the river in Lady Park are several unusual ferns: Adder's Tongue, Moonwort, Brittle Bladder Fern, and Limestone Polypody. It is here, now that the noise from the A 40 continues throughout the night, that one is most likely to hear the nightingale, once so common in these woods.

Lady Park is screened from the A 40, but at **Hadnock**, the road joins the river, its gaunt embankment obliterating the mediaeval chapel of St Michael. It was a hospice which stood near an important river crossing of the royal road leading through the Forest to Monmouth. Hadnock, one of the few Saxon place-names in the district, is a settlement which has Roman remains, and was once an important element in the lordship of Monmouth.

From here the river runs fairly straight towards Monmouth. On the right bank it passes **Dixton** Church, the foundation of an obscure Celtic evangelist called Tydwg (hence Llantydwg — Llantydwg'ston — Tydwg'ston — Dixton). It contains herring-bone masonry, as at Bredwardine, a Queen Anne royal arms, a royal head bell of c. 1450, a scraped font, a small broach spire, and white-washed plaster inside and out.

It has been flooded many times, and more recent inundations are recorded on brass tablets on the chancel arch:

1929	5' 6"
1947	6' 2"
1960	5' 2"

In 1852 the height was 4' 7", and the wardens had to pay the sexton 2/- extra for wading out to toll for the death of the Duke of Wellington.

The churchyard has some nice rustic tombstones. William Harris, who had been born during the Civil War, was one hundred years old when he died in 1745:

"Death took me off this Earthly Stage
When I had lived A good Age
I left behind me children seven
I hope to meet them all in Heaven."

Nearby is a Monmouthshire variant on the apocryphal Radnorshire "Him as was has gone from we/Us as is must go to he" which reads:

"Behold and see as you pass by
As you be now so once was i
As i am now so must you be
Prepare yourself to follow me."

It occurs, with slight variations, on the sanctuary floor (1708) and in the churchyard (1781).

Dixton has two other peculiarities. In 1860 the lay rector sued the vicar for trespassing in the chancel, a dispute which eventually reached the Court of Appeal; and it is in the diocese of Hereford, although the whole parish lies in Monmouthshire, an anomalous position which goes back to the twelfth century and correctly reflects many centuries of Anglo-Welsh rivalry.

The Wye enters Monmouthshire (now miscalled Gwent) at Hadnock, and for the rest of its course flows between that county and the Forest of Dean. Camden thought Monmouthshire very rich agriculturally, being able to support not only itself, but "the defects of the neighbouring counties". Thomas Churchyard, in 1586, was more impressed by the healthiness of the place: "Great health have they/In such sweet soyle who dwell". While Fuller, in 1662, called it an English-Welsh county and was interested in its "double badge of English relation". But, quite apart from its prosperity, healthiness or its political independence, many of those who live in it today prefer it above any other county, and would agree with John Fox's report to the Board of Agriculture in 1794 that it "is not surpassed, if it be equalled by any other part of this kingdom".

Monmouth, the county town, remained comparatively unspoilt until the twentieth century, and most visitors commended its approaches. The poet Gray, in 1771, wrote: "Monmouth, a town I never heard mentioned, lies on the same river, in a vale that is the delight of my eyes and the very seat of pleasure". Torrington, ten years later, thought the road from Gloucester the most beautiful he had ever seen; while Leitch Ritchie, in 1836, could find "no offensive contrast to the beautiful scenery by which it is surrounded".

He would not say as much today. The river, as it nears the bridge, finds itself hemmed in between a depressingly inappropriate industrial estate and caravan park on the left side and, on the right, the vast embankment of the

St Mary's Church, Monmouth.

The Author

The 1947 flood in Monnow Street, Monmouth.

Monmouth Museum

89

Wye Bridge, Monmouth and a man carrying a coracle.   *Monmouth Museum*

A40, brutally severing it from the town itself. These major blunders of the planners have deprived Monmouth of a river frontage worth looking at, and this is the only Wye town where that has happened. On the other hand, where the town has been allowed to grow naturally, it has retained much of its Georgian elegance and charm.

Urban sprawl has been limited by the liability to flooding of the surrounding open fields. This has isolated the mediaeval town in a natural green belt; and it is of some significance that the great flood of 1947, at its height, ringed the town, roughly on the line of the thirteenth century walls. The borough which grew up around the castle was ruled by Breton lords for the first two hundred years after the Conquest. It was closely linked with Hereford, in which diocese it lay, and it shared in the intellectual resurgence of the twelfth century. The Hereford metrical poet, Hue de Rotelande, dedicated a long poem to his patron, the lord of Monmouth, in which he described the castle as "rich in books both Latin and Romance".

There is little left of that castle where, in 1387, Henry the Fifth was born, but one of the few thirteenth century fortified bridges still guards the crossing of the Monnow. The bridge over the Wye is probably contemporary with that at Ross, although there was certainly a bridge near the site in the thirteenth

90

century. The remains of the priory with its fine oriel window, erroneously connected with Geoffrey of Monmouth, is now a Youth Hostel.

Monmouth's chief attraction is its Georgian architecture which grew up around a parish church designed by Smith of Warwick and a Shire Hall of great splendour, both built around 1730.

These buildings set standards which were further improved by the presence of the Somerset family just outside the town. At Troy House and Castle House (both c. 1673) they had introduced innovations which influenced craftsmen working on the lesser houses being built during the most prosperous period in the town's history, the two hundred years between 1660 and 1860. During these years Monmouth had a social season of plays, concerts, balls and race meetings which coincided with the assizes, and acted as a magnet for society over a wide area. The combination of lawyers, county families and industrialists from the Wye valley produced a variety of exemplary houses which led visitors to class the town as "well inhabited".

Smith of Warwick's church has been replaced by a rather dark building designed by G. E. Street, not an improvement, although Wilkinson's splendid spire was retained. The Monmouth bells are usually accredited to Henry the Fifth, who is said to have brought them back from Calais because they were too premature in celebrating his departure. They were recast in 1706 and the myth seems to have originated in a misreading of the inscription on one of them, "Habeo Nomen Gabrielis missi de Coelis". This is a fairly common inscription and other churches, reading Coelis as Calais, have acquired the same tradition.

Monmouth is luckier in its Nonconformist churches, though over the Monnow, the church of St Thomas has its original twelfth century chancel arch and was well restored in the nineteenth century. The Methodist church,

The Shire Hall, Monmouth with the statues of Henry V and C. S. Rolls. *Monmouth Museum*

built by a local architect in 1837 is probably the most pleasing place of worship in the town, while the Congregational church (1844) has the most imposing facade. One of the earliest post-Reformation Catholic churches was begun in 1793 and completed about a hundred years later. It has vestments and processional crosses of great interest.

Education has for a long time been one of the county town's major industries, and Monmouth School, founded by a local benefactor in 1614, monopolises a large area near the river, just as Monmouth School for Girls, founded in 1893, dominates the town from the other direction. But the core of the town is still its market place and the Shire Hall. It was in the latter that John Frost and his fellow Chartists were tried after the Newport demonstration, and although it is now more symbolic than functional, it retains a dignity which few other public buildings on the Wye possess.

Most of the eighteenth century tourists spent the night in one of the inns which surrounded the Shire Hall, but some slept on their boats. Bloomfield was one:

"The boat was moor'd upon the strand,

The wakeful steersman ready lay

To rouse us at the break of day.

It came — how soon! and what a sky

To cheer the bounding traveller's eye,

To make him spurn his couch of rest

To shout upon the river's breast . . . "

Torrington, who considered the Wye his favourite river, saw it from horseback on his first visit. On his second, after an expensive night in a Monmouth inn, he decided to risk a boat, and went aboard unenthusiastically at two o'clock in the afternoon, preceded by three boatmen and two servants "ladened with baggage like a Calais embarkation". No sooner were they out on the river than they were waylaid by other boatmen cajoling him into buying even more provisions.

When Nelson landed here in 1802, after travelling from Ross between banks lined with cheering spectators, he expressed surprise at being known at "such a little gut of a river". He thus became one of the few to make a derogatory remark about the Wye. But he was delighted to find, on top of the Kymin, a hill overlooking the town, the only memorial to the Navy in the kingdom. He came back on a second visit to inspect the names of the sixteen admirals, including his own, which are recorded on it. He breakfasted in the summer house there, thought the view one of the finest in the country, and was given the freedom of the borough. He also compiled a critical report on the state of the navy timber in the forest.

At the end of the century, Lady Llangattock, the mother of Charles Rolls, began to accumulate Nelson relics on a grand scale. In 1924 she bequeathed

Wye Bridge, Monmouth Weir and Troy House, c. 1740 from a picture by J. Smith.

Monmouth Museum

them to the town which, as a result, has one of the most comprehensive Nelson collections in the country, recently rehoused along with the local museum, in the old Market Hall.

Charles Rolls, who was brought up just outside Monmouth, did much of his early driving and ballooning around here. When he became the first man in England to be killed in powered flight, the town erected a statue to his memory in the middle of the market square. It was the work of Goscombe John and is greatly superior to the pathetic effigy of Henry the Fifth which overlooks him from the Shire Hall. The latter was the work of a local sculptor who made the victor of Agincourt look like a hypochondriac inspecting his thermometer. It was placed in the vacant niche in 1793.

Just below Wye Bridge was a weir and, beyond it, the River Monnow from which Monmouth takes its name. The Wye then turns away under the disused railway bridge (by Edward Finch of Chepstow) to be joined by another tributary, the Trothy. This stream flows past Troy House, a rather austere mansion, built by the first Duke of Beaufort at the same time that he was building Badminton and Great Castle House. From these fine houses, Monmouth, so long as it remained a pocket borough, was politically controlled.

"From hence, Wye," wrote Camden in 1610, "with many windings and turnings runneth down Southward, yielding very great plenty of delicate salmon from September to April".

The Naval Temple on The Kymin, Monmouth. *The Author*

CHAPTER SIX

Monmouth to Chepstow

FOR the rest of its course the river flows through a deep valley, thickly wooded on either side. It is accompanied for most of the way by the Chepstow road and, until recently, by the Wye Valley Railway, a line which was opened in 1876 with the deliberate intention of attracting visitors to "scenery which for its beauty, variety and grandeur could scarcely be surpassed". Inevitably, it was destroyed by Beeching and now, except for a stretch between Tiddenham and Tintern quarries, which still carries railway ballast, one of the most beautiful lines in the country has been demolished.

The road remains but, until 1828, travellers on foot reached Chepstow through Trelleck and along the high ground to St Arvans. This made access to Tintern difficult and the Reverend William Cole in 1746 described the descent "through narrow lanes and a most frightful precipice, all paved with stone, so that your horse can hardly manage himself to get down, much less with any one on his back". Eventually the Duke of Beaufort and others decided to sponsor a road along the valley and when it was opened Felix Farley's *Bristol Journal* acknowledged the debt that "persons in moderate circumstances" owed to these benefactors. Not only had the river tour become very expensive, a great deal of time was wasted waiting for boatmen, tides and service from the inns. The road made the traveller independent and saved him much frustration.

The absence of such a road until 1828 underlines the importance of the river to the industries which flourished along its banks from the sixteenth century onwards. Their remains have made this stretch a paradise for the industrial archaeologist. It abounds with well-documented sites of paper mills, leats,* embanked ponds, brass works, tramways, iron forges, copper works, quays, tinplate works, water mills and warehouses. Here men of enterprise used the natural resources of this beautiful valley, the fast-flowing streams, the charcoal, the timber, the ore, the coal, and the barge traffic with Bristol, to revolutionise industrial production.

The river turns away from Monmouth and high on the right bank, attended by a splendid yew, is **Penallt** church with its saddle-back tower. The chancel is lower than the nave, and the whole building gives the impression of being about to slide down to the river below, as one of the tombstones seems inadvertently to acknowledge: "I am not ded but sliping here". The original stone altar has been taken up from the porch and placed inside; there is a fine

*Open water courses conducting water to mills etc.

The Whitebrook Valley. *Wyedean Tourist Board*

dug-out chest, a Jacobean pulpit, a door dated 1539, a Queen Anne royal arms, and a communion table carved in 1916 by a refugee who was the chief wood-carver of Malines Cathedral. It is based on a stone altar at Ravenna. The barrel roof has attractive wooden bosses which have been repainted and restored, the gaps being filled with appropriate modern designs such as Sputnik I.

In the river below can be seen many of the millstones for which Penallt was famous and which, traditionally, were rolled down the slopes from where they were shaped on the hills above.

Penallt has one other claim to fame in the Argoed, a fine house dating from the sixteenth and seventeenth centuries. Here, in the 1860s, Richard Potter, chairman of the G.W.R., lived with his nine daughters. One of them, Beatrice, married Sidney Webb, and here, above the Wye, the early Fabians met, talked and wrote in the beautiful grounds of the house. Here Bernard Shaw, struggling with *Arms and the Man* and *Mrs Warren's Profession*, wrote some of his finest letters to Ellen Terry and here he met his future wife, "the Irish millionairess", who helped to found the London School of Economics.

When Shaw first came to the Argoed, he described the people he met as "very gentle, and clever and sly", but he loved the place and the company and, in one of his letters, wrote: "The God who made this country was an artist; he moulded his hills so that their lines run down into the valleys quite magically, and trimmed them with tufted woods so that not an acre glares, however warm the sunshine". Even the matter-of-fact Beatrice Webb, arriving from Scotland by an early train, was enchanted by "the exquisite beauty of the early morning spread over the Monmouth Valley".

At **Redbrook**, one of the great abandoned meanders of the Wye extends up to Newland then down the adjoining valley to meet the river five hundred yards downstream. Redbrook is an extensive village and when Archdeacon Coxe was here in 1799, he was impressed by the iron and tin works "which gave animation to the romantic scenery". Thanks to an abundance of charcoal and iron-ore, forges were active in the seventeenth century, while copper and tinplate were produced later. The tinplate works was closed on 14th December, 1961, and it was then the last factory in Britain, and probably in the world, to be producing tinplate by the old hand process. It had the further distinction of being the oldest steam-driven rolling plant in the world.

When the industry was at its height, Redbrook consisted largely of inns. Today it seems to be all garages. Above the village, at Highbury Farm, Offa's Dyke begins to thread the ridges of the English bank towards Chepstow. It is worth taking the road up the Redbrook valley, under the fine incline bridge, past the embanked ponds and leats, to Newland, a beautiful village with the finest church in the Forest.

With fewer meanders, the river reaches the **Whitebrook**, a stream which, falling steeply through a series of ponds, provided power for the mills which, from the eighteenth to the nineteenth century, produced high quality paper for export by barge to Bristol. They were built on the foundations of buildings used by the Tintern Wireworks Company, which had established a branch here in the sixteenth century. Many of the mill houses have survived, one with its drying shed still intact. They are memorials to an industry which used this beautiful valley without disfiguring it.

About a mile below Whitebrook the road crosses to the right bank. Bigsweir Bridge, a fine single-span structure has often been attributed to Telford, but was more probably the work of Charles Hollis, the designer of Windsor Bridge. It has a toll house and an abandoned station on the Monmouthshire side, and over on the left bank, Bigsweir House, an impressive building of c. 1740. The valley is overlooked from high on the same side by **St Briavels**, a village with an even older industrial history than Whitebrook. In the Middle Ages it supplied quarrels (bolts for crossbows) in vast numbers for military expeditions, and for castles throughout the border.

St Briavels Castle, with its majestic gatehouse, was once the administrative and judicial centre of the Forest. It was a favourite hunting-lodge of King John, whose visits at the beginning of the thirteenth century are traditionally remembered in the rhyme:

"St Briavels water and Whyral's wheat
Are the best bread and water King John ever eat."

The Whyral family lived in Newland parish, but the couplet more probably commemorates the diet in the castle gatehouse when it was in use as a notorious gaol. John Howard visited it in the 1770s, and found the prisoners huddled in a cold, bare hovel.

He had little good to say of the conditions but commended a certain Richard Milson who, every Sunday, sent the first helpings of his joint and a quantity of beer to each prisoner. It was a debtors' prison and, sixty years later, a correspondent to a local paper pointed out that the only prisoner there was Richard Milson's daughter, Helena. He appealed for donations to save her from the ultimate degradation, transfer to the Union Workhouse.

The walls of the gaol are scratched with the graffiti of the desperate and the defeated:

"Robin Belcher the day will come that thou shalt answer
for it for thou hast sworn against me 1671."

and

"My glas is roon tis time twas gone
For I have lived a great space
And I am weary of the place."

St Briavels castle is now more cheerfully employed as a Youth Hostel.

The parish church, basically cruciform, with a central tower, was restored in 1830 and 1861. The tower was taken down and rebuilt over the south porch and the chancel was reconstructed, but the impressive Norman arcade and font were left. There is a good Nicholson organ, the royal arms of Elizabeth II, and a stall carved with the Hunter's Horn, the symbol of the High Constable of the Forest. A fine brass chandelier, which was brought from Bristol in 1732, disappeared in 1861. Transport cost 9d for the boat journey from Bristol, and 1/- for carrying it from the barge to its place in the church.

Bigsweir marks another meander of the Wye, abandoned more recently than the one at Redbrook. Within a mile the river reaches **Llandogo**, a village of which Bloomfield approved:

"Delightful village! One by one,
Its climbing dwellings caught the sun.
So bright the scene, the air so clear,
Young love and joy seem'd stationed here;
And each with floating banners cried,
Stop friends, you'll meet the slimy tide."

At Llandogo the river becomes tidal, and the sight of the glistening mud banks at low tide usually dismayed the travellers. According to Leitch Ritchie, it also had "an effect on the moral character of the river". He was, presumably, concerned about the language of the boatmen, as shipping became more abundant.

Torrington thought Llandogo the most picturesque of all the villages, but Roscoe considered it had "a more picturesque appearance in pencil than reality . . . a near view does not add to its charms". Charles Greville went even further and wrote of the Wye as "a long slimy snake dragging its foul length through the hills and woods".

Downstream, large barges and trows sailed to Bristol, where that famous inn, the *Llandoger Trow* on the Welsh Back, commemorates the trade. Upstream, the smaller flat-bottomed boats were dragged by teams of men harnessed to the tow-rope. It was work which Charles Heath, the Monmouth writer, thought "none but British hearts would have the courage to call forth and persevere in". Many years later a master at Monmouth School described the desperate scene at a rapid: "The men bent forward and sometimes, if the barge happened to give a shear in a stream, they almost lay on the ground and waited till she could recover herself".

The whole village, with its *Sloop Hotel* and *Ship Inn*, had a nautical air. This is still prevalent in the old churchyard, neatly grazed by goats, which surrounds the Victorian church. There are anchors on some of the graves, and a large slab, commemorating Edward Madley (1776), has its curious verse written to fit the stone:

Llandogo in 1836 by W. H. Bartlett. *Brian Stevens*

"Though Boreas and neptunes waves
Have tost me to and fro in spite of both
By Gods decree I harbour here below
Whear at an Anchor i do Ride
With many of our fleet yet once again
We must set sail Our saviour Christ to meet."

There is also the inevitable river tragedy: "Elizabeth Morris . . . drowned on the Passage from Monmouth March ye 9th 1744 . . . likewise her son and daughter, Benjamin and Mary, with her".

The church, dedicated to St Oudoceus (hence the place name), contains the bell of *The William and Sarah*, one of the last Chepstow barges to trade on the river. The chancel is painted with texts, angels and flowers. There is an elaborate marble and alabaster reredos, with Moses, St Paul and some outsize doves, and a decorative roof over the nave. The sanctuary is pleasantly tiled, and in the south wall there is a simple white tablet to Anne Gallenga, the wife of the Italian patriot. The architect of this expensive church was J. P. Seddon, who also built Redbrook and Hoarwithy.

Charles Heath called Llandogo "a curious settlement" in 1800 and, seventy years later, it aroused even more curiosity when Lord Amberley, the son of Lord John Russell, settled at a house called Cleddon. He had already lost a safe parliamentary seat by advocating birth control, and he and his wife soon caused consternation in the village by advocating women's suffrage, abolition of the game laws, equal wages for men and women, a league of nations, concern for one parent families, and other radical causes. Lady Amberley taught in Trellech school, and took her son (Bertrand Russell) down to a Monmouth butcher to learn physiology.

They built a summer house, called Wordsworth's Hermitage, where they entertained and read aloud. John Stuart Mill was a frequent visitor, arriving by boat at Llandogo, and becoming their most impassioned reader, almost hysterical on one occasion when reading Shelley's *Ode on Liberty*. They also entertained the exiled Antonio Gallenga, who lived at Llandogo and eventually became a deputy in the Italian parliament, spending the winter in his constituency and the rest of the year by the Wye.

The Amberleys were avoided by the county families, but this did not affect their deep love of the valley. When they first saw it, Lady Amberley wrote in her diary, "We were quite enchanted with the wildness and the beauty of the place and A and I danced with delight". They died, as did their daughter, within three years of each other, and were buried, as they had wished, in the garden of their house.

On their death, the county received a further shock with the arrival at Cleddon of the Marquess of Blandford and Lady Aylesford. He was the son of the Duke of Marlborough, and her husband was a favoured friend of the

The Moravian Chapel at Brockweir. *The Author*

future Edward VII. They ran away together and caused one of the major Victorian scandals which culminated in the Prince of Wales challenging Lord Randolph Churchill to a duel.

Cleddon took its name from Cleddon Shoots, a series of waterfalls which brings the stream down 550 feet in a distance of half a mile. In its early course it runs through Cleddon Bog, an area notable for its wild flowers which include Sundew, Bog Asphodel, White Marsh Heather and Marsh Gentian. About a mile beyond Llandogo, at Coed Ithel, are the remains of one of the many weirs which crossed this length of the river while in the woods above, a seventeenth century blast-furnace, which used charcoal, cinders and iron-ore from the Forest, has been excavated.

Llandogo has suffered from unenlightened council development, something which cannot be said of **Brockweir**, the next village on the river. Between the two, the Wye runs fairly direct, the hills on either side thickly wooded, the Forestry Commission's territory having here spread over to the western bank. On the whole the lower Wye has been treated with more discretion than the upper, and only occasionally does one meet with an overdose of evergreens. There has been opposition to the planting of conifers in this area since the early nineteenth century when Fosbrook complained, "Will it never be known that firs in groups are like plumes on the graves of the Picturesque?" That was said in 1818, and one hundred and sixty years later it is beginning to sink in.

Brockweir is a real village, with a rushing brook, quays, Tudor houses, and a pleasant little Moravian chapel, complete with bell-cote, Gothic windows and art-nouveau glass. It was served by ferry until 1904 when the

101

present unimaginative bridge was built. It was the most important of the river ports, apart from Chepstow, and has a long history of trade and ship building. This has encouraged the publicans, and in 1820 it was reputed to have sixteen public houses. The Moravians did not set up a meeting where there was already a place of worship, and it is curious that the Church of England never built in Brockweir.

Before 1820 most of the boats built here were under one hundred tons, but in 1824 a ship of much greater size was launched at Monmouth and floated down to Brockweir for fitting out. The arrival of this ship, *The Duchess of Beaufort*, seems to have led to much activity during the next ten years when barques and brigantines of over 500 tons were built. The trade continued spasmodically until the coming of the railways, and there was still a Wye trow registered in 1925. One of the last to survive was *La Bella Helene*, a twin-screw steamer of 31 tons, which was found moored to the quay at Brockweir, completely engulfed in mud, in 1967.

After Brockweir, the river makes a horse-shoe bend and the valley widens as **Tintern** village comes into sight. This was, of course, the climax of the Wye Tour; but, before the abbey is reached, the river passes under a bridge which once carried a tramway from the Wire Works. It led to Tintern Station (now a showpiece of the Countryside Commission) and also, up a steep path, to the Devil's Pulpit. This magnificent viewpoint is, traditionally, the rostrum from which Satan canvassed the monks below to join the opposition. Close at hand is a fine stretch of Offa's Dyke.

In spite of the temptations from above, Tintern Abbey, founded by the lord of Chepstow in 1131, and rebuilt in the thirteenth century, throve. And it was the roofless remains of this second building, thickly coated in ivy and

Brockweir. *Wyedean Tourist Board*

Tintern.

surrounded by the hovels of the poor, which greeted the tourists as their boats passed the village.

The first reaction was one of dismay at the army of beggars waiting to receive them on the landing stage. They offered themselves as guides, and some visitors, including Gilpin, found them as interesting as the ruins. If they were all engaged, the landlady at the *Beaufort*, would, according to Charles Heath, "soon procure a little rustic to impart his store of information".

The next reaction was one of shock at the hovels surrounding the ruins and disappointment with the architecture, which most of the purists in the Picturesque found too formal. Gilpin, for instance, thought that "it does not make the appearance as a *distant* object which we expected. Though the parts are beautiful, the whole is ill-shaped". Roscoe admitted, however, that "the lack of enthusiasm we feel while on the outside, seems to serve only as a greater enhancement of the glory within".

Many people would feel the same today; and even that the hovels, the ivy and the beggars were preferable to the tarmac, the lavatories, the car parks, the information centres, exhibition halls, souvenir shops and other paraphernalia of the twentieth century with which the tourist industry is now saturated.

But once inside, the mood of the travellers changed. Archdeacon Coxe was filled with delight such as he had scarcely ever experienced, and Robert Bloomfield was equally ecstatic:

103

"Tintern, thy name shall hence sustain
A thousand raptures in my brain:
Joys, full of soul, all strength, all eye,
That cannot fade, that cannot die."

Words, for once, failed Torrington: "All description must fall short of its awful grandeur". But he was in no doubt about the way to enjoy it: "Bring wines, cold meat, with corn for the horses; (bread, beer, cyder and commonly salmon may be had at the Beaufort Arms), spread your table in the ruins; and possibly a Welsh harper may be procured from Chepstow". Welsh harpers soon outnumbered the natives and Webb, writing some thirty years later, thought the behaviour of many visitors had become blasphemous: "People who were indecorous enough to take their meals on consecrated ground . . . gave the place the appearance of a market".

As uninhibited as Torrington, was Kilvert who, at some risk, managed to scramble to the top of the walls so that he could look down into the choir, and then became interested in the wild flowers he found growing up there: scarlet poppies, white roses, purple mallow and yellow stone-crop. Roscoe had been equally enthusiastic, admiring the ivy, ferns, wallflowers and "a forest of ash and privet and wild intertwining roses".

Many of the early travellers had found the ruins lacking in solemnity and gloom. "It wants those yawning vaults and dreary recesses which strike the religious beholder with religious awe, make him almost shudder at entering them", wrote Grose, who would not have approved of the Department of Environment at all, "and the defects are increased by the ill-placed neatness of the poor people who show the building, and by whose absurd labour the ground is covered over by turf as even and trim as a bowling-green, which gives the building more the air of an artificial ruin in a garden than that of an ancient decayed abbey".

An occasional visitor foresaw that the silence so dear to the Cistercians would eventually be shattered by the pandemonium of the tourist industry. Wirt Sykes, the American consul in Cardiff, was one of them. In 1880 he gave thanks that Tintern was still sufficiently remote from London, "that excursion vomitting town", for "the soft note of the soda-water bottle to be seldom heard". Then, leaning against the wall of the *Rose and Crown*, he noticed an old yellow coach being used as a hen house and deciphered over the dashboard the ominous words THE TOURIST. Many of his fears have been realised and in summer Tintern tends to be too commercialised, too populous and too noisy. Wordsworth's "still sad music of humanity" is drowned by the transistor and the internal combustion engine. But in the autumn and in spring and under snow the magic of the abbey returns.

In its hey-day the Abbey owned estates on both sides of the river and as far afield as Norfolk. In the late thirteenth century it was producing the highest

Wye Tourists at Tintern.

Monmouth Museum

priced wool in the kingdom and had acquired privileges which gave it considerable control over the lower Wye. These included many hunting rights, free bark for their tannery, their own ferry, their own ships, warehouses, weirs, forges and, on some of their lands, authority "over gallows and judgement of life and limb".

At the dissolution, it was still wealthy. The abbot had six servants, a kitchen staff, tailor, barber and groom. There was a woodman, a ferryman, and four weirs (Plumweir, Ashweir, Ithelsweir and Walweir). When the abbey was closed, the land was sold to the Somersets, the bells and lead were removed by the royal plumbers, and the abbot was given an annual pension of £23.

It is perhaps ironic that the Cistercians, who sought peace in the remotest places, should have laid the foundations of the industries for which the village later became famous. Indeed, it seems likely that some activity continued after the monks had gone as, by 1565, patents had been granted to the Company of Mineral and Battery Works to draw wire from iron at both Tintern and Whitebrook. The works flourished and a hundred years later, Marmaduke Rawdon described the scene where the wire was being drawn into several sizes as "a curiosity worth seeing. The fire of the furnass where they melt the iron is soe great that, looking into the hole . . . itt looks like the sun in a hott day att noone".

Torrington was told by the agent in 1781 that he paid 1500 workmen from 18/- to 20/- a week. And Edward Davies, the Chepstow poet, described the scene at roughly the same time:

"Here, now no bell calls monks to morning prayer,
Daws only chant their early mattins there,
Black forges smoke, and noisy hammers beat
Where sooty cyclops puffing, drink and sweat;
Confront the curling flame, nor back retire,
But live like salamanders in the fire.

. . . .

Here smelting furnaces like Etna roar,
And force the latent iron from the ore;
The liquid metal from the furnace runs
And, caught in moulds of sand, forms pots or guns,
Oft shifts its shape, like Proteus in the fire,
Huge iron bars here dwindle into wire,
Assume such forms as suit the calls of trade,
Ploughshare or broadsword, pruning hook or spade."

A neglected memorial to all this industrial activity is the extensive churchyard at Chapel Hill, overlooking the abbey. The building is derelict, the roof fallen in, the doors torn from their hinges, the organ dismembered

Tintern Forge by Thomas Hearne. *Monmouth Museum*

and the windows broken. In the doorway are several flat stones, one of which commemorates Anne Allde, who died in 1670. "Shee buried three husbands" and the first of them lies beside her, "Francis Bradford, Clarke of the Wire Works". He was with her on his way to Whitebrook in 1657 when he fell headlong on his horse's neck. She cried for help, "soe he was carryed downe to Abbcy" whcrc, aftcr a wcck, hc dicd. Ouside, under the bracken and amongst the saplings and beer cans, are many fine tombstones, testifying to the company's prosperity and the size of its work force.

Another testimonial to Tintern's encouragement of both industry and tourism has, naturally, bccn thc numbcr of its pubs. John Taylor, in 1641, stayed the night in a "very cleanly wholesome Welch English Alehouse", and by the middle of the next century there were few buildings which were not taking in lodgers or providing some degree of hospitality.

Two of Tintern's sons have made names for themselves overseas: John Callice, one of the more notorious Elizabethan pirates, died in Barbary in 1587; and Colonel Lewis Morris, a Cromwellian cavalry commander, went to America at the Restoration to found an iron works at Tintern Falls, in what was to become Monmouth County in New Jersey.

Beyond Tintern, the river twists and turns between thickly wooded hills for the last time. The Wye tourist was expected to disembark and climb to the highest of them, the **Wyndcliff**. It was approached from Moss Cottage which had been built by the Duke of Beaufort's agent with Gothic windows, coloured glass and a table, made from a section of walnut tree, where travellers could refresh themselves before climbing the 365 steps to the top. These steps were recently restored by The Wye Valley Preservation Society. Although the number has been reduced to under 300, anyone with weak knees should approach the Wyndcliff from the car park at the top.

The woods along the bottom of the cliff were famous in the eighteenth century for nightingales. Mark Willett, a Chepstow printer, remarked that "the cliffs along the Wye, Piercefield Walks and the whole neighbourhood of Chepstow is generally admitted to abound more in nightingales than any part of this island; and that their notes are stronger and more harmonious than in other places. Some nightingales have lately been reared by Mr. Brookman, ropemaker, Chepstow, which has been considered a very unusual circumstance". The prevalence of nightingales is hard to reconcile with George Cumberland's observation at the same time that the woods were thick with foxes "and the valley at night filled with their howling". He may, of course, have been tone-deaf.

Fosbrook advised visitors to go to the Wyndcliff at sunrise or, at least, look at the view through a Claude, a pocket glass giving a sunrise effect. He considered "what a Cathedral is among churches, the Wyndcliff is among

From Wintour's Leap near Chepstow. *Wyedean Tourist Board*

prospects". But not everyone was so enthusiastic, and Thackeray, in his very long-winded account, thought the panorama too much to absorb, preferring the scene at the bottom. From the top, "the objects are too numerous to be distinct, and the eye wanders perplexed over such vast tracts of landscape".

Kilvert, who was always mentally comparing the lower Wye with Aberedw, was disgusted by the view from the Wyndcliff: "Any view would be spoilt by the filthy ditch which they call the Wye in the foreground, a ditch full of muddy water at the best of times . . . but now a scene of ugly foreshore and wastes of hideous mud banks with a sluggish brown stream winding low in the bottom between". He was equally disparaging about "the trick of Moss Cottage" and the stench of the place.

Most people disagreed with the critics and echoed the opinion of Thomas Roscoe: "The grouping of this landscape is perfect. I know of no picture more beautiful. Inexhaustible in details, boundless in extent, and yet marked by such grand and prominent features that confusion and monotony are completely avoided".

The Wyndcliff adjoined **Piercefield**, the last object of interest for the man of taste before Chepstow. This honeycomb of vistas, walks and grottos was devised by Valentine Morris in the eighteenth century. The walks had selected view-points, The Double View, The Platform, The Druid's Temple, as well as novelties such as a Cold Bath, The Lover's Leap, and swivel guns to produce echoes.

Sir Joseph Banks, who was here in the year before he sailed south with Cook, was "more and more convinced that it is far the most beautiful place I ever saw". But Torrington, a few years later, when Morris had sold the property to George Smith, thought the grounds could be better kept, that the well would be better employed as a wine cooler, and that the Lover's Leap was so well fenced that none but the desperate would attempt it. Roscoe was equally unenthusiastic about "so much puerility of design . . . grottos fabricated where grottos could not naturally exist . . . dilapidated giants . . . inscriptions calculated to make the unlearned stare and as sure to make the judicious grieve".

Torrington, who thought it an undesirable place to live, "being for ever on exhibition and in a glare", was particularly alarmed to see many of the elms in the avenue marked and numbered. John Wesley had similar fears in 1769 and asked "Must all these be burned up?" Their fears were realised and when Torrington came back in 1787 he found that most of them had been destroyed.

One of the most popular figures in British mythology has been Joseph of Arimathea, because of his association with the Arthurian quest for the Holy Grail, the platter in which he had collected Christ's blood. Amongst the many legends that grew up around him was the belief that he married a daughter of

Longinus, the centurion who pierced Christ's side, and who was, in turn, a natural son of Julius Caesar. Leland, in 1540, had noted without comment that one of Chepstow's towers was called Longine, but it was left to Anne Elfe, a Chepstow poetess of limited ability but boundless imagination, to establish him at Piercefield:

> "Where art and nature now combine to please,
> Longinus dwelt, and there he first found ease:
> Piercefield he called it, there conviction first
> Subdued his pride and on his reason burst."

This was probably one better than the theory of Elizabeth Smith, "Piercefield's pious, soul-illumined maid", who wrote in the style of Ossian and decided that Llywelyn ap Gryffidd should stain it with his blood:

> "Pierc'd with a spear ingloriously he'll fall,
> Whence future times that spot shall Piercefield call."

The grounds are now Chepstow Racecourse.

Back on the river, the travellers encircled the Lancaut Peninsula, with its church of St James. It is now a ruin and its fine lead font, one of only about thirty in the country, is in the Lady Chapel of Gloucester Cathedral. Lancaut church was the last building the Wye tourist was expected to notice before reaching **Chepstow**, which Wyndham, one of the most conscientious writers on the picturesque, thought "so uncommonly excellent, that the most exact critic in landscape would scarcely wish to alter a position in the assemblage of woods, cliffs, ruins and water".

The town was first admired from the water, then the travellers disembarked and the boatmen were paid off. Bloomfield was delighted with everything, as usual:

> "When first we hail'd, then moor'd beside
> Rock-founded Chepstow's mouldering pride,
> Where that strange bridge, light, trembling, high,
> Strides like a spider o'er the Wye."

And, unlike most travellers, who were glad to see the last of their boatmen, he sent his back with gratitude:

> "Pollett farewell! Thy dashing oar
> Shall lull us into peace no more . . .
> And happy be the hearts that glide
> Through such a scene, with such a guide."

Torrington was not so effusive. He arrived when the wool fair was at its height, the maypole "well hung round with garlands", plenty of puppet shows, balance masters, and Welsh squires intoxicating themselves. He found the town "very neat" and admired the wild flowers growing amongst the ivy on the castle walls, "Valerian, Fox-glove and red and white Lady Tire, a most

110

Chepstow Castle.

Wyedean Tourist Board

glittering flower". But he was more impressed by the Chepstow women, "having fair skins with very long eyes and noses".

Chepstow, like Monmouth, has had an abundance of pubs, many of them linked by name to the rivers from which came so much of their trade: *The Sailor's Tavern, The Severn Trow, The Ship, The Steam Packet, The Blue Anchor, The Chepstow Boat, The Lord Nelson, The Mermaid, The Wye Packet House, The Hope and Anchor* and *The Nelson Arms*, to name but a few. Even today Chepstow makes more use of its riverside than most of the Wye towns, and has a dock area which is still in use.

Much of its early importance as a sea port arose from the Bordeaux wine trade, the lords of Chepstow having been granted authority to collect the prisage on it in the thirteenth century. But Chepstow was also a tourist attraction in its own right. The superb position of the castle, the priory church, and its place as the terminus of the Wye Tour brought many visitors from east and west.

The first attraction was usually the castle, one of the earliest to be built after the Conquest, containing innovations in the design of its mural towers

Chepstow.

Wyedean Tourist Board

and shooting slits. It was extended and strengthened over the next five centuries, so that it was still partly habitable at the beginning of the nineteenth.

Information to the visitors was imparted by the Williams family, especially Mrs Williams, who died at the age of ninety in 1778. Her mother had lived to be one hundred years old and her grandmother one hundred and three. Charles Heath found her a valuable source of information because she had known the women who looked after Henry Marten, the regicide. He had been imprisoned at the Restoration in the tower, now known as Marten's, where he lived for some years with his family. Southey greatly overrated his discomforts when he wrote:

"He never saw the sun's delightful beams
Save when, through yon high bars, he poured
A sad and broken splendour . . . "

Torrington, who found his guide "very voluble and ignorant", was interested chiefly in a chimney which was glazed inside and did not need sweeping.

Visitors went next to the church which, like St Briavels, had originally been cruciform with a central tower. In 1700 it had suffered the same fate as Hereford when the tower collapsed and was rebuilt at the west end. There were two nineteenth century restorations; one in 1841, when Wyatt ruthlessly removed the Norman side aisles, chancel and transepts to provide an extra 600 seats; and another in 1891 when Seddon and Carter rebuilt the chancel and south transept.

The church is impressive inside, with its fine Norman arcade which Wyatt spared, and the very good columns inserted in the 1891 rebuilding. The organ is one of the few pre-Civil War instruments still being used; there are two fonts, one Norman, the other fifteenth century; the works of the 1775 church clock are on display; and the royal arms of Queen Victoria adorn the gallery of the bell-tower.

There are also two fine monuments, both coloured. The first (1549) supports the effigies of the second Earl of Worcester and his wife in their coronation robes and coronets. The second (1620) shows the twice-married Mrs Clayton, lying full length with her two small husbands praying above her and her twelve children kneeling below. The tomb of Henry Marten was removed from the chancel to the west end by an eighteenth century Royalist vicar. It contains a long epitaph beginning: "Here September the Ninth in the year of Our Lord 1680 was buried A True Englishman" and containing a verse in which the first letters of each line spell his name. A nobler character, imprisoned in the castle during 1654, was the Royalist bishop, Jeremy Taylor.

Torrington amused himself reading the inscriptions on the tombs, especially enjoying one concerning John Leask, a Chepstow sea captain, which was "a happy mixture of religion and prophane; about Neptune and Admiral

Christ". George Lipscombe copied out the whole inscription in 1802. It is very like the one in Llandogo churchyard:

"The blusterous blasts and Neptune's waves,
Have tost me too and fro:
In spite of all, by God's decree
I harbour here below,
Here I am anchor'd with many of our fleet
But we shall sail again our Admiral Christ to meet."

The town itself flows steeply down to the Wye from the West Gate. Bridge Street, with its bow windows and fine individual houses, is especially pleasing, and would be even more so if the traffic could be removed, as has happened in Hocker Hill Street. The steepness of the streets was well described by the Reverend Edward Davies:

"He, who by land would enter Chepstow town,
Must quit his horse and lead him gently down:
The long descent so rugged is and steep,
That even post-boys here for safety creep;
The sloping road demands our utmost care,
Hawker, when living, never gallop'd here.
Cats with sharp claws, and nanny-goats in dread
Descend the shelving street and cautious tread.

. . . .

In this snug town good meat and drink abound
But, strange to tell, there cannot here be found
One single inch of horizontal ground . . . "

Burrow's *Guide*, in 1903, described Chepstow as "one of those quaint and unprogressive towns which have somehow managed to escape the effects of nineteenth century progress". Alas, this is no longer true, and the twentieth century has caught up with a vengeance. The centre of the town around the war memorial has recently been debased by an influx of the usual brand of cheap provincial supermarketechture. Monmouth's centre has suffered a similar misfortune, but whereas Monmouth has the Shire Hall to maintain some dignity, Chepstow's centre is dominated by the brual black and white tower of Barclay's Bank, appropriately adorned with a large iron eagle which looks as if it has just polished off any objectors to the design.

The whole depressing area is flooded with traffic trying to get out. But although the centre, once ringed by an almost continuous circuit of pubs, has been sacrificed, the castle, the parish church, and even the station, have been retained along with the bridges.

The station came in for criticism when it was opened in 1876, because the platform was three feet below the carriages, and invalids and the fat had to be

114

hoisted in by porters, "regardless of decency . . . and the object of unchaste remarks". As a result, 41 men with jacks managed to raise both platforms nearly two feet in two operations, in which not a pane of glass was broken nor a single stone dislodged.

Chepstow Bridge goes back to the thirteenth century when, like Monmouth, it formed one of the boundaries of the Forest of Dean. Leland found it a ruin, and it then became the joint responsibility of the counties of Monmouth and Gloucester, and a hazard which few travellers forgot. Edward Davies, again, is the best witness:

"The startled traveller gives God his thanks
When pass'd with safety o'er the rattling planks.
This tottering bridge fills animals with fear,
Hard is the task to drive them over here.
The sturdy ox, obedient to the goad
Here quarrels with his driver and the road,
Unwilling moves in his elastic path
That bends and springs beneath him like a lath.

. . . .

The drunken clown alone, when passing here,
Sings and reels on, insensible of fear."

It was the considerable rise in the tide which set the problems for the builders of Chepstow's bridges. John Rastrick built the present one in 1816, and Brunel the great tubular railway bridge in 1852. The latter was so unusual that it soon became one of the sights of Chepstow.

The G.W.R. had completed the London to Gloucester line in 1845, and the South Wales Company was formed soon afterwards to carry the line to Milford. A gap was left over the Wye, and passengers had to cross it on foot or by coach. Brunel was asked to link the two sections with a central span of 100 yards and a clearance of 50 feet above the highest known tide. His bridge was supported on cast-iron cylinders, filled with concrete, and sunk 48 feet into the rock, while the suspension chains were held rigid by girders. It cost over £65,000 and was strengthened by British Rail in 1962.

In 1911, the river was the scene of one of the more bizarre events in its long history when Dr Orville Owen, the author of *Sir Francis Bacon's Cipher Story*, in six volumes, decided to tie up the loose ends in his theory by finding the manuscripts of Shakespeare's plays. He calculated that they had been hidden in 66 boxes near Chepstow. After a fruitless search in Peglar's Cave, he decided they must be in the Wye, so a coffer dam was built and 24 workmen began to burrow into the tidal mud. The boxes were not found but,

Dredging the Wye for the Bacon manuscripts.   *Chepstow Museum*

undeterred, Dr Owen had the castle cellar excavated in 1920, and four years later dug around the grotto in Piercefield Park. The vital evidence is still missing, though the river excavation did uncover the footings of a very early bridge.

Even the enthusiasm of Mr and Mrs S. C. Hall began to wane during the two miles beyond Chepstow; "They are miles of anti-climax; low meadows and sides of mud mark the parting of the fair river, in mournful contrast with its beauties passed . . . It would seem as if the river had wearied of perpetual beauty, or was unwilling to grace its gigantic sister, in whose embraces it was to be lost".

But the tidal Wye, from Chepstow downstream, had one other property which was denied to it elsewhere; it was reckoned to cure the bite from a mad dog. James Parry, in his memoirs written in 1741, describes how a pack of hounds, attacked by a mad dog near Ross, were hurried to Chepstow to be dipped in the rising tide. As late as 1863 a girl was rushed from Monmouth to be dipped, and the practice continued until even later in the century, in spite of the fact that, as early as 1831, there had been objections that washing so much madness into the Wye would make the fish dangerous to eat.

In this last stretch, the Wye flows sluggishly past a sewage works, Bulwark, the Army Apprentices' School, an iron-age bridgehead camp, and then under the western section of the Severn Bridge, to lose itself in the river

117

The old bridge, Chepstow.

Chepstow Museum

which was born beside it on the bleak slopes of Plynlimon. Here, the equally bleak mouth of the river, with its ruined island chapel of St Twrog, separates two of the oldest crossings over the Severn into Wales and the Marches.

The New Passage, from Black Rock, was probably the old Roman crossing place and older than the Old Passage from Beachley to Aust. Each had several boats, using sail when there was a wind, otherwise they were towed across by men in a rowing boat. The passage rarely caused anything but frustration and fury. John Wesley suffered as much as anyone, a typical experience in 1748 involving a wait of five hours at the New Passage before being told that the delay was due to the boatmen being afraid to admit that they were afraid to cross. He rode to the Old Passage to find that the boat had just left. Similar trouble occurred on almost all his many crossings during the rest of the century.

Until the Severn Bridge was built, most travellers had time, while waiting for the ferry, to look back on the river they were leaving. Wordsworth must have thought of some of the lines composed above Tintern Abbey whilst so engaged: "I began it upon leaving Tintern, after crossing the Wye", he wrote, "and concluded it just as I was entering Bristol in the evening . . . Not a line of it was altered and not any part of it written down till I reached Bristol".

118

The dominant impression of that poem is one of tranquillity:

"Once again
Do I behold these steep and lofty cliffs,
That on a wild secluded scene impress
Thoughts of more deep seclusion; and connect
The landscape with the quiet of the sky . . . "

And tranquillity will still be one of the memories of the traveller as he leaves the river today, tranquillity which accompanies it as it moves through all the variations in the scenery, from mountains and sheep, past orchards and cattle, to the forest and deer of Dean. So it is perhaps appropriate, in conclusion, to look back briefly on some of the accessories of the Wye, elements which have become almost synonymous with it and a part of its insignia — timber-framed houses, cider, perry, Hereford cattle and, above all, salmon.

Part of the poster for the opening of Chepstow Bridge, 1816.   *Chepstow Museum*

FORM OF THE
CEREMONY
FOR OPENING
CHEPSTOW BRIDGE,
On Wednesday, 24th July, 1816.

Company to assemble in the Square at One o'Clock.

THE PROCESSION.

A PAIR OF COLOURS.
ENGINEER & SURVEYOR.

Workmen in Divisions according to their Order, walking two and two.

A PAIR OF COLOURS.

Appendix I   Buildings

Very roughly, the Wye rises amongst the Upper Silurian rocks, travels through the Lower Silurian around Builth and, at Llanstephan, enters the Old Red Sandstone. It continues through this until it reaches Symonds Yat and a short stretch of Carboniferous Limestone. Then, well before Monmouth, it re-enters the Old Red Sandstone which extends as far as Tintern, where Carboniferous Limestone and the Keuper Marls take it through Chepstow to the Severn.

To a certain extent, the geology of the river has determined the way in which building has been carried on. Lack of limestone for mortar has always made stone building difficult. Similarly, the presence of large quantities of oak made timber-framed construction easy and cheap. Celia Fiennes, in 1696, called Hereford "a pretty little town of timber buildings". Her words could have described all the Wye towns from Rhayader to Chepstow, as any eighteenth century watercolour will confirm.

Cruck building (the use of large timbers curving from near ground-level to support the roof by means of a ridge beam) was widely adopted in Radnorshire, as was the combined byre and dwelling of the Welsh long house. Herefordshire and Monmouthshire also used cruck building, but paid less attention to the long house. The decline of timber-framed building was due partly to bad maintenance, partly to the growing scarcity of oak, and partly to the substitution of brick in-filling for wattle and daub.

Oak, and timber generally, became scarce owing to the huge quantities consumed by the iron forges, and the lack of any national policy of replanting. In the seventeenth century, John Beale bemoaned the fact that "the iron mills have devoured our glory and deflowered our groves". And in 1640 the Grand Jury of Herefordshire complained that "the iron mills . . . have byne a general distruccon of trees, tymber and Coppice Wood . . . insomuch that the said Cittie is already in great want and scarcity of wood".

It was not only the iron forges that deflowered the groves. Chepstow was exporting up to five thousand tons of bark a year in the late eighteenth century, and the great demands of the Navy for the best crooked timber added to the scarcity. Pepys and Evelyn tried to encourage re-afforestation, and their efforts were supported locally by the Marquess of Worcester and Lord Scudamore, who always claimed to be "a great preserver of woods against the day of England's needs". But when Nelson reported on the Forest of Dean in 1802 he found little to commend and was appalled by its neglect.

Brick eventually took over from timber-framing, but it was not much used on the lower Wye until the seventeenth century. It was expensive, and there was a shortage of craftsmen. When Monmouth School was built in 1614, bricklayers had to be brought from London and until bricks could be mass-produced and transported easily, their use was the privilege of the wealthy. The Scudamores could afford a brick house at Holme Lacy in the sixteenth century, but it was not until the eighteenth that the Monmouth gentry could build houses like Lloyds Bank or Cornewall House.

The pitch of a roof varies with the climate and the weight of the material it carries. In Radnorshire and Monmouthshire the beautifully graduated stone tiles needed strong timbers to support them. In Herefordshire, thatch was more often used until, towards the end of the eighteenth century, farmers discovered that straw was more useful mixed with manure, and technical advances in slate quarrying made that material more easily available.

Stone had, of course been used in castles, and the demolition of many of them after the Civil War made it plentiful. Castle House, in Monmouth, was built from the great square stones of the castle gate. At the same time (1673) the Marquess of Worcester was building Troy House on the lower Wye, while on the middle Wye at Holme Lacy, Lord Scudamore was pulling down "the good old house built with brick" and replacing it with "a fair house of freestone" (1671).

External plaster was the mediaeval answer to damp. It protected the walls from rainwater which, before the days of guttering, ran straight off the roof. Dixton Church, which still has the original pitch of roof, was not scraped by Victorian restorers and has retained its plaster inside and out. Although it is more subject to flooding than most Wye churches, its walls are completely free from damp.

Generalisations about building techniques in such a varied area as the Wye Valley are dangerous, but most new fashions were introduced upstream by wealthy landowners like the Somersets (who used brick in their castle at Raglan), the Scudamores and the Cornewalls. From their great houses at Monmouth, Holme Lacy and Moccas, innovations such as plaster ceiling decoration were disseminated into the houses of the lesser gentry. And, outside the towns and the industrialised lower Wye, the lesser gentry were, almost without exception, engaged in the cultivation of the land.

Appendix II   Agriculture

From the source of the Wye to Hay, there is very little arable land but abundant pasture. After Hay, the valley widens through the rich Hereford-shire farmland, and this continues as far as Kerne Bridge. From here it is again confined between hills, this time thickly wooded, which continue until the river reaches the Severn at Chepstow.

These geographical divisions have, naturally, dictated the pattern of farming and, to a certain extent, it can be traced in the varying designs of the old wooden farm gates. In the upper valley, Welsh pastoral life persisted long after more permanent communities had evolved south of Hay. Under the Welsh system, the shepherds took their flocks to the *hafod*, or summer pasture, where they lived in temporary dwellings of turf and timber until winter, when they moved down to the *hendre*, the lower, more sheltered quarters of their kindred.

As the Welsh laws, which regulated this way of life, lost their hold, the kindred began to disintegrate and individual families moved away to establish more permanent farms with small irregular fields on the empty hillsides. Even in the sixteenth century, Leland noticed that the Welsh lived "sparsim" rather than "vicatim", and the movement was accelerated by the demand for wool.

Sheep farming increased in importance in the fourteenth century, largely through the Cistercians with their extensive sheep walks, but also through the growth of manorial flocks. By 1372 both the manor of Clifford and the lordship of Hay had many sheep and, by the sixteenth century, Radnorshire wool had been highly praised by Leland, and Tintern was producing the most expensive wool in the country.

Even so, the farming in the upper Wye Valley was less efficient than lower down, and Malkin was appalled by what he saw in Radnorshire in 1804. The standard of husbandry was deplorable, "the appearance of the farms . . . impoverished and hungry", while fertility was kept down by slovenly management, local prejudice and indolent habits. In spite of this they seemed to live well enough: "The people, almost without exception, live upon meat, oatmeal, milk, butter and cheese. They eat great quantities of meat but bread somewhat sparingly . . . Most of their land is used for grazing, a little for tillage, less still for gardening, and for growing of fruit trees hardly at all".

In Herefordshire the picture was very different. It was pacified within a few years of Hastings and, except in Archenfield, Norman manorial organisation took contral of its rich red earth. Moreover it was enclosed early. Leland described it as such in the sixteenth century and John Clark, in 1794, thought that "in general it seems to have been enclosed from the forest state, and this accounts for its crooked fences and narrow lanes".

Unlike Radnorshire, Celia Fiennes found it looking like "a Country of Gardens and Orchards, the whole county being very full of fruit trees . . . thick even in their corn fields and hedgerows". Forty years earlier John Beale had described Herefordshire as the orchard of England, and remarked on the hedges being "enriched with rows of fruit trees, pears or apples". A good deal of this was "kernel fruit", raised direct from seed and not grafted.

Appendix III   The Orchards

Camden had commented on the Herefordshire orchards and added that the owners made "such vast quantities of cider, as not only serve their own families (for it is their common ordinary drink) but also furnish London and other parts of England". Cider was, of course, a mediaeval drink, and the Monmouth accounts show 60 gallons being sold in 1256 for 2/-. Perry was even older and, according to some authorities, was preferred by the Romans. But John Beale considered it a woman's drink: "Pears make a weak drink fit for our hindes, and is generally refused by our gentry as breeding wind in the stomach".

When Defoe came here he was surprised that ale was unobtainable in the county's inns, but delighted to find the cider "so good, so fine and so cheap that we never found fault with the exchange". Its fame was not confined to Herefordshire as Edward Davies of Chepstow acknowledged in 1786:

"No better cider does the world supply
Than grows along thy borders, gentle Wye.
Delicious, strong and exquisitely fine,
With all the friendly properties of wine."

By mid-seventeenth century it was becoming known abroad as "The White Wine of England", but it has never quite attained the universal acclaim that John Phillips, the Herefordshire poet, expected:

"Where the British spread
Triumphant banners, or their fame has reached
Diffusive, to the utmost bounds of this
Wide Universe, Silurian cider borne
Shall please all tastes and triumph o'er the vine."

It has remained closely linked to the county for many centuries, an aspect which is emphasised by the Cider Bible in the chained library at Hereford. This bible, in which the words "strong drink" are translated as "cider", has been attributed to Nicholas Hereford, the Lollard who was Wycliffe's chief assistant translator.

In the eighteenth century, the Herefordshire farm labourer's perquisites included 2 to 3 quarts a day in winter, 3 to 4 in summer, and 6 quarts at harvest. It was a custom which was abused when huge imports of French wine after the end of the Napoleonic wars left the farmers with a surplus which they could only get rid of to their labourers.

But it was the quality of the cider, rather than the quantity, that was important: and Thomas Dineley was told in 1684 by the vicar of Dilwyn that the old in Herefordshire were not "bedridden or decrepit as elsewhere, but for the most part lively and vigorous". Next to God, he ascribed this to the orchards, "that are not only the ornament but the pride of our county".

Evidence for this geriatric vigour is usually provided by the story of the twelve Morris dancers, celebrating a visit of James I to the Golden Valley, whose combined ages came to twelve hundred years, while the music was played by four men whose ages totalled four hundred and twenty-three. Fuller referred to "this nest of Nestors" but ascribed their "vigorous vivacity" to the good air rather than cider or God.

The cultivation of the apple has a long tradition of folk ceremonial. John Aubrey watched fires being lit in the fields to bless the apples on Midsummer Eve; while around Brinsop, the burning of the bush on New Year's Eve involved a fire on the twelfth ridge and men standing in a circle, singing very slowly the dirge "Holloa auld cider" and bowing nine times as low as possible. Apples were also connected with St Peter and St Swithun, and had to be blessed on their feast days for the harvest to succeed. There was also a tradition that Herefordshire labourers, before drinking cider in the fields, should allow a few drops to fall from their costrel to the ground as a libation.

The biggest threat to the apple orchards was taxation, and when the tax on cider was repealed in 1766, thanks largely to the efforts of Sir Velters Cornewall, a song was written in celebration which included the following verse:

"A Health to all our members let's drink in merry vein,
To Rockingham and Pratt, let's fill it up again.
Likewise to Pitt and Dowdeswell, we'll stretch our throats still wider
And all the Moccas hills shall echo back Old Cider.
   Then let the merry bells all ring
   And music sweetly play
Let shining bonfires blaze around
   To close this joyful day."

When Sir Velters was buried in 1768, twelve women walked in procession, carrying apple boughs.

An apple was the badge of the old Herefordshire regiment, and the freedom of the city was always presented in a box of apple wood. This happened to Nelson when he was made a freeman. It has even been suggested that the ballflower ornament, that curiously-named fourteenth century motif, which occurs so frequently in Herefordshire churches, may have been based on the bud of the apple blossom. If this is so, it is appropriate that it should have survived longer as a decorative detail in this county than in any other.

The long tradition of apple and pear growing has given to the names of many of the trees an evocative, time-honoured charm: The Stire, The Hagloe-crab, The Woodcock, The Cockagee, The Moyle, The Gennet-Moyle, The Pawson, The Fox Whelp (supposed to keep for forty years), The Ten Commandments, The Brandy Apple, The Loan Pearmain, The Yellow Musk, The Huffcap, The Dymock Red, The Taynton Squash, The Bosbury Scarlet and, most famous of all, The Red Streak. The finest tribute to them is T. A. Knight's *Pomona Herefordiensis*, published in 1811, with superb colour plates of 26 apples and 6 pears.

Appendix IV   **Hereford Cattle**

The Wye is at its most enchanting when the orchards are in blossom, or in the autumn, when the apples lie in pyramids beneath the turning leaves. but just as no traveller on the river could fail to taste its cider, so would it have been impossible for him, after the eighteenth century, to ignore the unmistakable features of Hereford cattle.

John Speed, in 1627, noted that "the Climate of Herefordshire is most healthful and the soyle so fertile for corne and cattle, that no place in England yieldeth more or better condition". He was writing shortly before the Tomkins family was to find itself on the losing side in the Civil War, and a long time before its members were to embark on the production of the most famous of all breeds of cattle.

In 1723, Richard Tomkins, of King's Pyon, some six miles north of Hereford, left his herd of cattle to his sons, naming each animal separately. Amongst them was the cow "Silver", left to the fourth son, Benjamin. Using Silver, Benjamin and other members of the family eventually produced a herd containing three distinct strains, grey, red with mottled face, and red with white face. It was the last of these which became dominant, as William Marshall noted in 1788, when describing their qualities: "Full of heart and vigour . . . the countenance pleasant, cheerful, open, the forehead broad; the eye full and lively; the horns bright, tapering and spreading; the head small; . . . the coat neatly haired, bright and silky; its colour a middle red with a bald face; the last being esteemed characteristic of the true Hereford breed".

Cobbett called them "certainly the finest and most beautiful of all horned cattle", and by 1816 they were being exported to the United States. In 1846 the first volume of *The Hereford Herd Book* was published and thirty-two years later the Society was formed which took over control of the breed. Today there are few countries where Herefords do not flourish. They reached Argentina in 1876 and a hundred years later there were ten million there. They extend from Sweden to New Zealand, and from Canada to the Straits of Magellan, but they will ever be associated with the county which gave them their name, and will always look their best knee-deep in the Wye on a hot summer afternoon.

125

Appendix V   Salmon

Giraldus, writing in 1188, noted that "the salmon of the Wye are in season during the winter, those of the Usk in summer, but the Wye alone produces the fish called umber, the praise of which is celebrated in the works of Ambrosius . . ." "What," says he, "is more beautiful to behold, more agreeable to smell, or more pleasant to taste?" Giraldus's enthusiasm for the umber or grayling is a useful reminder that the Wye produces other fish than salmon, and that there were times when unrestricted netting very nearly removed them from the river altogether.

The lamprey was another fish to be greatly appreciated in mediaeval times, and in 1256 the lord of Monmouth spent the huge sum of over £4 on sending 21 of them to London. These curious creatures can be seen on the sandy gravels around Breinton in March, standing on their heads to scoop a depression for their eggs. Shadd, a fish well known to the Romans and Egyptians, is rare in all British rivers except the Severn and the Wye. They arrive in April and sometimes travel as far as Builth to lay their eggs. It was alleged in 1560 that the building of Redbrook weir doubled the price of shadds in Monmouth, where they were bought to relieve the poor during Lent.

Eels are common, and elvers have always been a delicacy, caught in the spring, and boiled and pressed into cheese-like jelly which can be sliced and fried. Other fish which live in the Wye include chub, dace, roach, pike, perch and gudgeon. And, although trout are more numerous in the tributaries, there is an old adage that

"When the bud of the alder is as big as a trout's eye
Then that fish is in season in the River Wye."

But salmon have always taken pride of place in a river which is subject to frequent flushing from its many tributaries. They can ascend during spates and rest in the deeper pools when the river falls; and the long stretches of clean gravel in the upper reaches are ideal for spawning. This almost perfect environment has meant that over the centuries there have been endless disputes about the best time, place and method of destroying them.

Fluellen probably gave the Wye its greatest early publicity when Shakespeare made him compare Henry the Fifth with Alexander the Great, and Macedon's river with Monmouth's. He could not remember the name of the river in Macedon but "it is called Wye at Monmouth . . . and there is salmons in both". When the monasteries were closed, the crown found itself in possession of considerable fishing rights and the Tudors were well aware of their value. Elizabeth I, for instance, when disposing of the lands of Monmouth Priory, specifically retained to herself "the tithes of salmon and other fish taken or to be taken in the waters and rivers within the parish of Monmouth".

Edward I had attempted to protect salmon parr, and as early as 1307, Roger Carey was outlawed for netting Wye salmon, and his accomplice had his nets burnt, but thereafter matters deteriorated and no real efforts were made to protect the fish. Great numbers of weirs made things worse and, although Camden in 1610 agreed with Giraldus that Wye salmon were at their best in winter, Fuller by the end of the century was maintaining that the important thing about them was that they were in season all the year round.

Rowland Vaughan, a contemporary of Camden, had put the case against the weirs: "Take pity on a whole country groaning under the burden of intolerable weirs . . . the river of Wye is so weired and fortified as if the salmon therein (on pain of imprisonment) had been forbidden their usual walks". He had seen the river at Chepstow "swollen with a sea of salmon" and maintained that, until the weirs restricted their movements, "a Herefordshire servant would surfeit on fresh salmon as oft as a Northamptonshire man on fat venison".

His appeal fell on deaf ears, and fishing, throughout the year, by rod, net and spear continued into the nineteenth century. Ross hotels specialised in salmon fry, and fishermen in Monmouth maintained that parr were not salmon at all, but the young of a fish called the Blue Cock.

Little was done to regulate affairs until the Salmon Fisheries Act was passed in 1861, and one of its effects was to spark off riots by those who maintained that the river was an open one. In this they had the sympathy of many magistrates and great numbers of breeding fish were killed around Rhayader. The coming of the railways increased the slaughter as the fish could more easily be sent to London.

This state of affairs divided the river into three factions. In Radnorshire and the upper reaches, it was claimed that, as the salmon bred in their waters, they had every right to kill them. Around Chepstow and the lower Wye it was maintained that, as salmon arrived from the sea, no one could prevent them being caught there. The less fortunate inhabitants of the middle stretch were happy to kill anything that survived the slaughter at either end.

It was from the middle Wye, rather naturally, that the first efforts to save the salmon came. The Wye Preservation Society was founded in 1862 with Sir Velters Cornewall of Moccas as chairman. It concentrated on the protection of spawning fish and ignored the question of netting. Alexander Miller was appointed superintendent water-bailiff, and he and his sons organised netting on such a scale that they practically emptied the river of fish.

In 1866 the Wye Board of Conservators was formed under the Duke of Beaufort with power to issue licences and levy rates. In the following year Frank Buckland became Inspector of Fisheries and probably did more to save the Wye as a fishing river than anyone else. He carried on a campaign against netting, introduced 700 Rhine salmon, and co-operated with Miller in the construction of salmon passes and ladders. He also did much to discredit the legend that indentures once contained a clause stating that apprentices should not be made to eat salmon more than three times a week. He offered a reward of £5 to anyone who could produce any such document and none ever appeared.

But netting continued and fish became scarcer. This made it less profitable and a Wye Fisheries Association was set up which began to buy netting rights from fishermen who were glad to be rid of them. In 1901, the Duke of Beaufort, who had leased his rights on the lower Wye, sold them to the crown on condition that they were leased to the Association. Control then became much easier, but even in 1913, it was estimated that nets caught ten times more fish than did rods, although rod licences produced over £1,800 and nets less than £500. The last netting rights were bought in 1924, and it is now illegal above Brockweir and strictly controlled below it.

The salvation of the salmon has been admirably described by H. A. Gilbert in *The Tale of a Wye Fisherman*, and the Wye River Authority publishes a useful *Guide to Angling Facilities*. It is thanks to a few enlightened men that it is now once again a great fishing river. And great throughout its length, with many famous pools: The Nith, Locksters, Adam's Catch, The Cowpond, The Dog Hole, Martin's, The Quarry, Colman, and Cadora; and linked to them such salmon flies as Dusty Miller, The Usk Grub, Jock Scott, Thunder and Lightning, and The Wye Besom.

Thackeray thought Wye salmon should be eaten with a little salt and a slice of bread. It was then an unforgettable joy. Edward Davies was precise about its preparation:

"Adown the back the cook the fish divides,
Takes out the chine, in pieces cuts the sides;
Plung'd in the coldest water lets it lie
Till the pot boils, and foaming, bubbles high;
Then, piece by piece, he souses in the fish,
Which, boil'd ten minutes, makes for kings a dish.
A salmon whole, well dressed, I never saw,
O'er boil'd without, but in the middle raw:
But thus divided you no hazard run,
For every part alike is nicely done.

. . . .

Unlike the flabby fish in London sold,
A Chepstow salmon's worth his weight in gold;
Crimps up delightful to the taste and sight,
In flakes alternate of fine red and white.

Who would not wish with Chepstow swains to dine,
Where salmon swims, the second time in wine!
Few other rivers such fine salmon feed,
Not Taff, not Tay, not Tyne, nor Trent, nor Tweed."

Appendix VI   **Canoeing**

Almost the only way in which the traveller today can emulate the eighteenth century tourist on the river itself is by canoe. It is still, probably, the best of all ways of enjoying the Wye but, for those embarking for the first time, there are a few points that should be remembered:

1. The rights of anglers should be respected, the Country Code should be obeyed and, unless using a recognised site, permission to land and/or camp should be obtained in advance.

2. It should be realised that the river can always be dangerous and that some places are more dangerous than others.

a. Glasbury—Hay. Canoeists are asked to leave before 1600 hours as a later departure interferes with the fishing. If the river is low some of the rapids cannot be shot without damage to canoes. There is a weir (Wyecliff), 5 miles below Glasbury, which must be negotiated carefully close to the right bank, while there are many rocks and obstructions below Hay Bridge.

b. Bredwardine rapid, about 20 miles below Glasbury, has a large boulder in the middle which can be hazardous as this is a "sharp" rapid.

c. Monnington Falls, always dangerous to barges in the past, is still difficult. In high water the river flows over a rock reef to the right of the island, but when it is low the falls can be shot by going to the left of the island where the water flows fast down a funnel. This is a rapid which should be inspected first.

d. After passing the weedy shallows at Bridge Sollers, there are few hazards until about 4 miles below Mordiford where there are three islands. Unless the main stream is followed close to the right bank, the canoe will have to be carried over ledges between the islands.

e. Kerne Bridge should be approached with caution as the rapids cause eddies, and hidden boulders extend for about a quarter of a mile.

f. About half a mile before Huntsham Bridge is reached there is a rapid with a pointed rock which has accounted for many canoes.

g. Symonds Yat rapids are probably the most enjoyable of all but they should be inspected first. The head is close to the left bank and the stretch continues for about a quarter of a mile.

h. Between Monmouth and Redbrook there are several large boulders (depending on the height of the water) which can be dangerous.

i. Below Bigsweir Bridge there is an interesting rapid to the left of the island where the canoeist should beware of overhanging trees.

j. Beyond Llandogo the tidal mud makes landing difficult and between Tintern and Chepstow it is impossible. Tintern should be left within one hour of high water and landing at Chepstow should be made on the right bank at the steps between the bridges. Beware of flotsam on this last stretch.

Finally, it should be remembered that, even at its most placid, the Wye can be dangerous. There is a long tradition that the river will exact an annual sacrifice. Mrs Leather, in *The Folk Lore of Herefordshire*, recalled an occasion when a boy was drowned near Ross. Somebody remarked that his brothers would now be careful to keep away from the banks. An old man, overhearing this, said "Let 'em go, let 'em go, no one else will be drowned this year, the river has had its due".

Herefords at the Monmouthshire Show. *D. H. Jones*

Bibliography

General
Barber, J. T.: *A Tour through South Wales.* (1803).
Borrow, George: *Wild Wales.* (1862).
Byng, Hon. John: *The Torrington Diaries.* (1781-1794).
Churchyard, Thomas: *The Worthiness of Wales.* (1587).
Cobbett, William: *Rural Rides.* (1821-1832).
Defoe, Daniel: *A Tour through the whole Island of Great Britain.* (1724-1727).
Dineley, Thomas: *The Account of the Official Progress of His Grace Henry, the First Duke of Beaufort, through Wales.* (1684).
Fiennes, Celia: *Journeys.* (1685-1703).
Fuller, Thomas: *The Worthies of England.* (1662).
Giraldus, Cambrensis: *The Itinerary through Wales.* (1188).
Hadfield, Charles: *The Canals of South Wales and the Border.* (1960).
Hall, Mr and Mrs S. C.: *The Book of South Wales.* (1861).
Hussey, Christopher: *The Picturesque. Studies in a Point of View.* (1927).
Jones, P. T.: *Welsh Border Country.* (1946).
Leather, Mrs E. M.: *The Folk-Lore of Herefordshire.* (1912).
Leland, John: *Itinerary.* (1535-1543).
Lewis, Samuel: *Topographical Dictionary of Wales.* (1842).
Lipscombe, George: *Journey into South Wales.* (1802).
Malkin, B. H.: *The Scenery, Antiquities and Biography of South Wales.* (1804).
Moir, Esther: *The Discovery of Britain. The English Tourists.* (1964).
Pennant, Thomas: *Tours in Wales.* (1804-1813).
Plomer, William ed.: *Selections from the Diaries of the Reverend Francis Kilvert.* (1870-1879).
Riddelsdell, H. J.: *The Flora of Gloucestershire.* (1948).
Roscoe, Thomas: *Wanderings and Excursions in South Wales.* (1844).
Skrine, Henry: *Two Successive Tours throughout the Whole of Wales.* (1798).
Sykes, Wirt: *Rambles and Studies in Old South Wales.* (1881).
Wade, A. E.: *The Flora of Monmouthshire.* (1970).
Wesley, John: *The Journal.* (1735-1790).
Whitehead, L. E.: *Plants of Herefordshire.* (1976).
Wyndham, H. P.: *A Tour through Monmouthshire and Wales.* (1774).

The River
Bloomfield, Robert: *The Banks of Wye. A Poem.* (1811).
Bradley, A. G.: *The Wye.* Illustrated by Sutton Palmer. (1910).
Cash, J. A.: *The River Wye.* (1952).
Cohen, I.: *The Non-Tidal Wye and its Navigation.* (Transactions of the Woolhope Club, 1956).
Drayton, Michael: *Poly-Olbion.* (1590).
Dreghorn, W.: *Geology explained in the Forest of Dean and the Wye Valley.* (1968).
Farr, Grahame: *Chepstow Ships.* (1954).
Fletcher, H. V. L.: *Portrait of the Wye Valley.* (1968).
Fosbrook, T. D.: *The Wye Tour or Gilpin on the Wye.* (1818).
Gibbings, Robert: *Coming Down the Wye.* (1942).
Gilbert, H. A.: *The Tale of a Wye Fisherman.* (1929).
Gilpin, Rev. W.: *Observations on the River Wye.* (1770).
Heath, Charles: *The Excursion down the Wye.* (1799).

Hutton, E.: *The Book of the Wye.* (1912).

Hutton, J. A.: *Rod Fishing for Salmon on the Wye.* (1920).

Ireland, Samuel: *Picturesque Views on the River Wye.* (1797).

Potts, W. H.: *Roaming down the Wye.* (1949).

Ritchie, Leitch: *The Wye and its Associations. A Picturesque Ramble.* (1840).

Searle, E. J.: *The Rivers of Monmouthshire.* (1970).

Shaw, C. R.: *Fifty miles from Hereford to Redbrook.* (Ms. for canoeists in Hereford City Library 1948).

Twamley, L. A.: *An Autumn Ramble by the Wye.* (1838).

Willet, Mark: *The Stranger's Guide to the Banks of the Wye.* (c.1839).

Willan, T. S.: *River Navigation in England.* (1936).

Wye River Authority: *Guide to Fishing Facilities.* (N.D.).

Places

Bannister, A. T.: *The Cathedral Church of Hereford.* (1924).

Bannister, A. T.: *The Place-Names of Herefordshire.* (1916).

Beazley, E. and Howell, P.: *The Companion Guide to North Wales.* (1975).

Bradney, Sir J. A.: *A History of Monmouthshire.* (1904-1913).

Clark, Arthur: *The Story of Monmouthshire.* (1962).

Coxe, W.: *A Historical Tour through Monmouthshire.* (1801).

Davies, E.: *Chepstow. A Poem.* (1811).

Davies, E.: *A Gazetteer of Welsh Place-Names.* (1958).

Duncumb, J.: *Collections towards the History and Antiquities of the County of Hereford.* (with Continuations 1804-1912).

Fairs, G. L.: *A History of the Hay* (1972).

Hart, Cyril: *The Industrial History of Dean.* (1971).

Hart, Cyril: *Archaeology in Dean.* (1967).

Hart, Cyril: *The Verderers and Forest Laws of Dean.* (1971).

Heath, Charles: *Monmouth.* (1804).

Heath, Charles: *Tintern Abbey.* (1803).

Howse, W. H.: *Radnorshire.* (1949).

Jones, T.: *Brecknockshire.* (1805).

Kissack, Keith: *Monmouth. The Making of a County Town.* (1975).

Nicholls, H. G.: *The Forest of Dean.* (1858).

Pevsner, N.: *Herefordshire.* (Buildings of England, 1963).

Price, John: *An Historical Account of the City of Hereford with some remarks on the River Wye.* (1796).

Royal Commission on Historical Monuments: *Herefordshire.* (3 vols 1931).

Smith, Peter: *Houses of the Welsh Countryside.* (1975).

Verey, David: *Gloucestershire.* (Buildings of England 1971).

Victoria County History: *Herefordshire.* (1908).

Waters, Ivor: *About Chepstow.* (1952).

Waters, Ivor: *Piercefield.* (1957).

Waters, Ivor: *Inns and Taverns of the Wye Valley.* (1976).

Williams, Rev. J. A.: *Radnorshire.* (1815).

Index